The Anatomy of Skiing:

▶ from intermediate on

The Anatomy of Skiing:

(Revised)

from intermediate on

By
Richard J. Sanders, MD

Illustrated by
Rick G. Delmendo

 Published in the United States by Random House, Inc., New York and in Canada by Random House of Canada Limited, Toronto. Originally published in another version by Golden Bell Press in 1976.

Cover Design by Barbara Green

Library of Congress Cataloging in Publication Data

Sanders, Richard J.

The Anatomy of Skiing, (Revised) from intermediate on.

Reprint of 1976 edition published by Golden Bell Press
Reprint of 1979 edition by Vintage Books, a division of Random House
2003 edition published by Eastwood Printing and Publishing
1. Skis and skiing-- Physiological aspects. 2. Anatomy, Human.
I. Title.
ISBN 0-9746781-0-4
Manufactured in the United States of America

DEDICATION

To

Kevin, Amy, and Michael

David, Jane, Debbie, and Steve

and to Jo

Also by Richard J. Sanders, M.D.

Carcinoids of the Gastrointestinal Tract
1973

The Anatomy of Skiing and Powder Skiing
1976

The Anatomy of Skiing
1979

Thoracic Outlet Syndrome
A common sequela of neck injuries
1991

CONTENTS

The Anatomy of Skiing (Revised): from intermediate on

By Richard J. Sanders, MD

Preface xii
Introduction xvii

Part I: Basic Skills

1. Bare Essentials 3

The ski versus a flat board 3
Ski construction---The anatomy of a ski 4
Camber 4
Flexibility 4
Side-cut 6
Length and width 7
Torsion 7
Choosing a ski 8
4 basic skills 8
Gentle vs. steep slopes 9
Safety 9
Recreational vs. racing skiing 10

2. Anatomy of a turn 13

A. Initiation of a turn 13

1. Edge change 13
2. Stem turns 13
3. Parallel turns pivoting 17

B. Completion of a turn 17

1. Skidding 18
2. Carving 20

3. Knees and Shoulders–an Overview 25

Shoulder rotation 25
No shoulder rotation (Anticipation) 26
Knee Angulation–Knee Flexion 29
Pressure release 30
Banking and hip angulation 31

4. Edging 33

Knee angulation 34
Knee flexion(bending) 36
Hip angulation 36
Banking 39

5. Edging: How to use it 43

Sideslipping and sidestepping 43
Stopping 47
Skidding and carving 51
Wedge (Snowplow) and stem turns 53
Uphill and downhill stem 54
Edge control with the wedge 55
Garlands 57

6. Balance 59

Fore/Aft balance 59
Weight forward versus backwards 61
Hands and Poles 63
Balance between the two feet 63
Weighting the downhill (or turning) ski 63
Minor points: 64
Advancing your uphill ski 64
Touching the knees together 64

7. Pressure Control 65

Pressure release by down-UP movement 66

Down motion for pressure release 69
Leg retraction 71
Pressure release over a mogul 75
8. Rotation 79
Foot rotation 80
Shoulder Rotation with the Turn 82
Shoulder Rotation Before the Turn--Anticipation 82
No Shoulder Rotation (continuous anticipation) 84
Exercises to maintain shoulders facing downhill 86
Hip rotation 88
Knee rotation 89
Steering 90
9. Poles and arms 91

Part II:Putting it all together

10. Gentle smooth slopes 97
Where to learn 98
Order of learning 98
Short skis 99
Edge control 100
Traverse with knee angulation 100
Steering 100
Parallel turns 101
Rolling edges--crossovers 101
The easy turn--pure carved turn--banking 102
Parallel turns with rotation 105
Pivoting both feet 105
Pressure release--unweighting 105
Basic parallel turn 106
Wedeln--get some rhythm 108
Better parallel turns 110
Preturn–end of one turn is start of another 110
Anticipation 112
Banking 114
Combining skills 115
Minor points 115
Weighting the uphill ski 115
Lifting your inside ski 116
Advancing the uphill ski 117

Knees touching 117
Leaning forward 117

11. Steep slopes 119

Short radius turns 120
Anticipation 121
Weight forward 122
Pole plants 122
Pre-turns and checking 123
Shoulders and skis in opposite directions 124
Compression 124
Foot thrust forward and jetting 125
Commitment 125
Difference between checking and pre-turns 127
Hip Angulation 127
Carving and skidding 128

12. Bumps 133

Even pressure on your skis 134
Forward/backward balance 135
Pressure control 137
Down-pressure release 139
Turning on crest of a mogul 141
Leg retraction 142
Differentiate down-unweighting from leg retraction 142
Routes and Paths 143
Ski troughs vs. avoid troughs 144
Ski the banks 144
Ski the mogul crests 144
Don't forget to breathe 145
Moguls on gentle vs. steep slopes 145
Pole plants 146
Anticipation 147

13. Powder 149

Pack vs. powder 150
Shallow vs. deep powder 151
Equipment 152
Flexibility 153
Binding position 155
Wide skis 155
Ski length 156
Getting started in deep powder 157

Rhythm 157
Pivoting in powder 158
Knee angulation 158
Subtle points 159
Foot advance 159
Flexion-extension or compression turns 160
Banking 161
3 rules of powder 162
Weight equal on both feet 162
Weight centered, not too much forward 162
Complete turns by carving 164
Steepness of slope 165
Gentle slopes 165
Steep slopes 165

Part III: Extras

14. Difficult Conditions 169
Ice 169
Crust 170
Crud 172
15. Equipment 173
Boots 173
Skis 175
Bindings 178
Poles 179
16. Appendix of exercises on the slopes and before a mirror 181
Knee angulation and shoulders downhill 181
Wedeln exercise 181
Sideslipping exercise–Garlands 182
Knee angulation in front of a mirror 183
Pressure release (Unweighting) exercises 183
Leg retraction 183

Glossary of Ski Terms 185

PREFACE

This book is for intermediate skiers who would like to ski better. Once you can stand on skis, move down gentle slopes, and stop, you have entered the broad level of intermediate skiing. You can stay at this level a long time or you can improve your skiing to advanced levels in a short time. Progress is attainable without much difficulty if you understand just a few basic principles of skiing. Skiing should be fun; learning to improve your skiing can also be fun if you know which parts of your body to focus on.

In an earlier book, "The Anatomy of Skiing", I presented a primer on skiing. It included a description of the basic skills of skiing and how they are used at the beginner, intermediate, and advanced levels. The present book relies on the same basic skills, but presents them in a more condensed fashion.

Why another ski book? For simplification. Although the basic skills of skiing haven't changed, ways of explaining them have improved. While many books describe how to ski, readers often find it difficult to transfer what they read to what they do on the slope. The essence of this book is embodied in four chapters which deal with the each of the four major slope conditions: gentle slopes, steep slopes, bumps, and powder. The nitty gritty details of precise execution in each of these situations is spelled out in a logical fashion. The reader should find the organization very user friendly.

The Anatomy of skiing: from intermediate on tells you how to edge your skis, plant your poles, and hold your shoulders. It explains why you have trouble on steep slopes and moguls AND tells you exactly where to focus your concentration to improve. Where I disagree with a few of the "rules of skiing" which have been around for a long time, I explain the reasons. The book is aimed at recreational skiing, not racing. There is a difference.

The what, how, and why of learning

In learning to ski, as in learning other skills, there are three levels of knowledge: Knowing **what** to do; knowing **how** to do it; and knowing **why** you should do it a specific way. In the course of learning, some students can observe and follow; knowing what to do is enough for them. They do not have to be told how to do it or why; just seeing it is enough for them to grasp the movement and perform it (the concept behind "The Inner Skier" by Tim Gallaway).

Many more of us cannot learn by simply knowing what to do; we need more help. We can observe an expert ski down a slope, but our brain is unable to process all that is reaching it. The brain cannot send the right messages to our muscles to perform what was seen. We need to be told exactly **how** to execute the main actions and secondary actions.

Finally, even after having been told precisely how to perform a skill, some people are skeptical, particularly when what is told to them disagrees with other things they have previously learned or heard. When we have doubts about whether or not our teachers are correct, we need verification, proof, or further explanations as to why we should learn a particular skill in a prescribed way.

Doubts can inhibit performance. If we are concerned that what we are learning might be incorrect or unimportant, our ability to concentrate on it suffers and we don't learn it well, if we learn it at all. Logical explanations that alleviate our concerns permit us to concentrate all of our attention on the matter at hand. Our ability to learn improves considerably.

A major difference between teachers of any sport is the elements of that sport that are emphasized; what is of primary importance and what is secondary. There are many things to be learned; which do you do first and which can wait until later? While this book describes the detailed skills required to become a better skier, it also clearly separates major from minor points and what to concentrate on at progressive stages.

Who should one believe? Ski instructors sometimes

emphasize different aspects of skiing, and it is not unusual for instructors to contradict one another. There are many little "rules" in skiing that are taught by friends, instructors, and other skiers. Who is right? Actually, under appropriate circumstances, each may be right. The explanation is that under different slope and snow conditions requirements change. The technics needed under certain conditions may be unimportant in others. This book addresses such problems. It stresses the order in which to learn your skills. It also recognizes that in learning to ski better, it is hard to focus on more than one thing at a time.

Acknowledgements

My thanks to Alan Bush, Dr. Ed Goldson, Dr. Stan Gottlieb, and Dr. Rick Abrams, for their review of this manuscript and critiques.

INTRODUCTION

As you ride a ski lift and observe the skiers on the hill below, you can easily separate good from novice skiers. The good skier moves straight down the fall line, knees flexed, skis together, skis moving in unison, legs turning from side to side beneath the hips, a quiet upper body flowing with each turn but not rotating, and arms and poles held comfortably in front and to the side. The entire body moves in rhythm.

The novice skier is quite a contrast: More time is spent traversing the hill than descending it; knees are straight, seldom flexed; turns are made with the skis apart, rarely moving together; shoulders, arms and poles rotate from side to side with each turn instead of remaining fixed, facing down the fall-line; and a continuous rhythm is sadly lacking.

At the intermediate level, skiers focus their attention on their skis and legs. Skiing tends to be rigid and forced with little relaxation. There is a hesitancy, a resistance to letting the body commit to a turn. At the advanced level, these features have changed: skiing is smooth and fluid; turning is continuous and flowing; and the entire body is a picture of relaxation, elegance and grace. What has happened!

Intermediates ski primarily with their lower bodies. The upper body is a passive participant and serves mainly for balance. In contrast, advanced skiers have learned to control the lower body so well that the lower body performs automatically. The upper body becomes a major player. Turns are made not only with the legs but with the whole body--legs, hips, torso, and shoulders--all working in unison and all flowing continuously in a constant pattern of movement. There is a regular rhythm to the turns. The advanced skier looks like a dancer swaying back and forth to an endless song. Turns do not begin and end; they are simply a part of a constantly flowing motion.

The differences between intermediate and advanced skiers is what this book is about. You can progress from intermediate to advanced levels of skiing in a very short time by concentrating on just a few basic fundamentals of skiing.

The main features to focus on as you strive to improve your skiing are:

Knee angulation--control speed with your knees
No shoulder rotation--stop rotating your shoulders through turn
Pressure Release --lift your weight or release the pressure from your feet to permit quick, parallel turns

There is much more to skiing than this list. In **The Anatomy of Skiing: from intermediate on,** I stress knee angulation as the most important method of edge control. However, two other methods of edge control must also be learned: hip angulation and banking. For adult skiers, knee angulation is the more difficult skill to develop because it requires knee flexion; and knee flexion, bending your knees, is an action that takes some skiers months or years to perform. But once you've learned to flex and angulate your knees, the other methods of edge control can easily be added.

Different skills are used under different slope conditions; split second timing of one action after another is essential; proper use of your arms, poles, upper body, pressure control, and appropriate weight transfer are all skills you must eventually develop. However, if you can learn each skill separately, you will have mastered the hard part. Putting the skills together with rhythm and precision will not be difficult once you can feel and perform the individual motions. Knowing which actions to concentrate on and in what order to learn them will help you master difficult slopes with confidence and finesse.

How to use this book

While this book can be read from cover to cover, each chapter in sequence, it can also be read a little at a time. The material is presented in such a way that each chapter has one or more messages and can be read alone.

The first nine chapters talk about the principles of skiing and individual skills. The meat of the book is in Chapters 10-13 which discuss the four main ski slope conditions and how to ski them: Gentle slopes, steep slopes, bumps, and powder. If you are wondering how to begin, try Chapter 10, Gentle Slopes. This will introduce you to all of the ideas in skiing. From there, if you want to read more about a specific skill, go to one of the first nine chapters which focus on single ideas.

If you already are a good intermediate skier and wish to develop the finer points to advance to expert skiing, the chapters on steep and bumpy slopes may be the place for you to start.

There are some redundancies in the book. If you read the book from front to back, it will become apparent that a few points are repeated throughout the book. However, the regular appearance of "knee angulation" and "shoulders facing downhill" is the constant reminder to those who read short portions at a time that these are "the essence" of advanced skiing.

Part I

The Basic Skills

Chapter 1
Bare Essentials

Ski vs. flat board
Ski construction---The anatomy of a ski
- ***Camber***
- ***Flexibility***
- ***Side-cut***
- ***Length and width***
- ***Torsion***

Choosing a ski
4 Basic skills
Gentle vs. steep slopes
Safety
Recreational vs. racing skiing

There are a few basic bits of information that all skiers should know. If you have skied a few times, you probably know most of these. If you are not familiar with them, look at them for a quick overview of the mechanics of skiing.

The ski versus a flat board

Understanding how a ski works and how it is controlled can be helpful in learning to ski well. The basic difference between a ski and a flat board is in the use of the edges of the ski. A flat board placed on its broad side on a ski slope will slide down the steepest path it can find to the bottom of the hill, accelerating as it goes. Lying flat on its bottom, a ski will do the same thing–head straight downhill, out of control. But, if a ski is positioned on one of its edges, the edge will dig into the snow slowing down the ski. In fact, you spend far more time skiing on the edges of your skis than on the bottoms. Knowing how to control the edges is the essence of skiing.

Ski Construction-The Anatomy of a Ski

The edge of the ski is designed with a curve that runs the full length of the ski called the side-cut of the ski. The tip and tail of the ski are wider than the center **[Figure 1]**. When the ski is turned onto an edge, the tip and tail rest on the snow, but the mid-section is suspended in air. When standing on a ski that is positioned on its edge, your weight and pressure in the mid-section pushes the suspended center of the ski down until it rests on the snow. At that moment, the entire edge of one side of the ski is contacting the ground and the ski is now curved, not straight as it had been when resting with its bottom against the flat slope **[Figure2]**. By skiing on the edge of the ski, your path will follow the curve in the ski creating a gentle turn. Following this edge is called carving.

Camber: Most skis are manufactured with a bow along the bottom of the ski between the tip and tail. This is seen by laying a ski on a hard flat surface and noticing that the tip and tail touch the surface, but the center of the ski is suspended in air. This upward curve is called the ski's camber. When you put your weight or pressure in the center of a ski, you flatten or reverse the ski's camber **[Figure 1]**. When you lighten or release your pressure, the center of the ski springs back, tending to lift you up. The speed of regaining it's camber when the pressure is released is one of the main factors in describing a ski's responsiveness and performance. Manufacturers are constantly changing the materials in the center core of a ski to improve the ski's performance by shortening its responsiveness time and giving you a quicker rebound following pressure release on a ski.

Flexibility: The two basic characteristics of a ski are flexibility and side-cut. Flexibility refers to how stiff or soft (flexible) a ski is. When you press with your hand against the middle of a ski as it is standing in an upright position, a soft ski will bend several centimeters quite easily, while a stiff ski will be difficult to bend more than one or two centimeters. A flexible ski tends to vibrate and wiggle more than a stiff ski, particularly at faster speeds, therefore stiff skis are desirable on flat cruising runs. In

Anatomy of a ski

Figure 1

A) The tip and tail of the ski are wider than the mid-section (or the waist). This is called the ski's side-cut. **B)** Most skis are built with an arc in the center called the ski's camber. **C)** When the tip and tail are suspended and the center of the ski weighted, the camber is reversed.

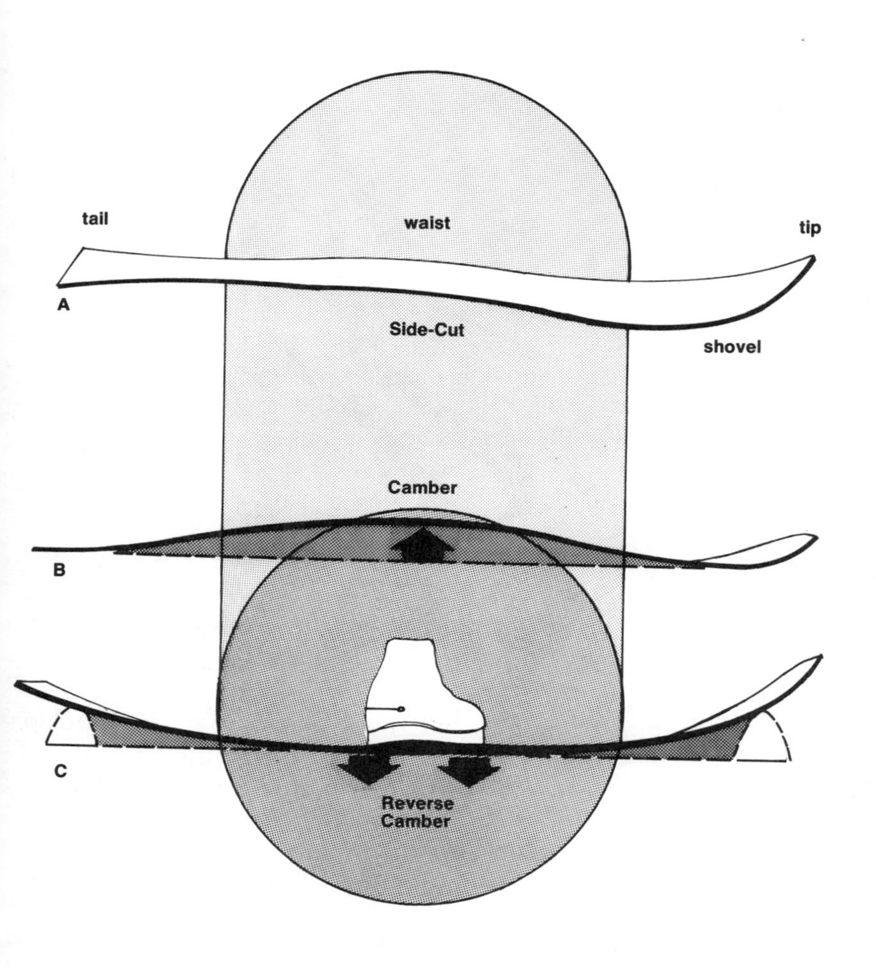

Figure 2 **Carving with reverse camber**

The skis are turned on their edges so that the tips and tails contact the snow. The mid-section is suspended until the skier's weight pushes the ski downward. This reverses the camber of the ski, producing a curve. A turn that follows this curve is a "carved turn" as discussed in Chapters 2 and Chapter 5.

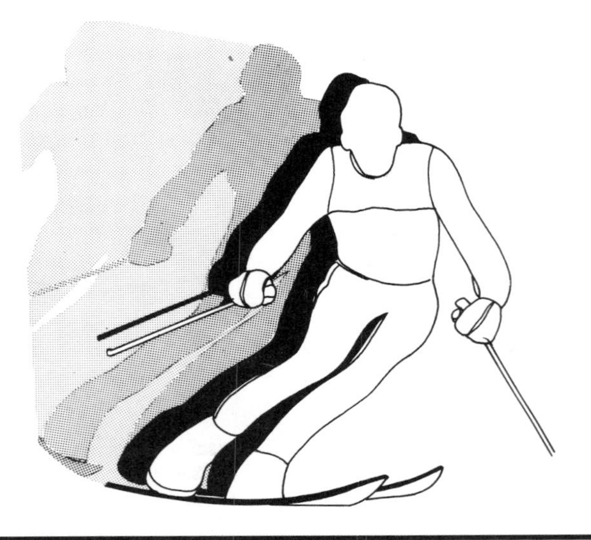

contrast, a flexible ski makes skiing in deep powder snow easier than a stiff ski because the flexible ski helps you keep your tips from diving deep into the snow and makes turning easier.

In bumps or moguls, stiffness in a ski permits quicker and sharper edge control and faster turns, but the tip and tail of a stiffer ski is apt to get caught when you hit the side of a sharp mogul. A ski with a flexible tip can bend and let the ski rise over the mogul. Ski manufacturers have tried various combinations of flexibility and stiffness in the same ski by making the mid-section stiff and the front and back sections flexible. The portion of the ski that is flexible versus the portion that is stiff is a variable among manufacturers as well as among the different models of the same manufacturer.

Side-cut: The side-cut of a ski is the design that makes the tip and tail of a ski wider than its mid-section (the waist). The tail and the tip (actually the shovel) can be just a few millimeters wider than the waist or they can be 2-4 centimeters wider (as in the parabolic or shaped ski). The purpose of side-cut is to suspend the center of the ski when it is set on its edge in a turn. When the ski lies flat on the snow, the side-cut is of no significance because the entire bottom of the ski is resting on the snow. However, when you set the ski on edge so the bottom of the ski is suspended off the snow, the tip and tail of the ski contact the snow while the waist of the ski is suspended in air (because of the side-cut). As you exert pressure on the ski with your weight, the center of the ski pushes outward until it hits the snow. If the side-cut is minimal the resulting curve in the ski will be small. If the side-cut is bigger, as demonstrated by the parabolic or shaped ski, the resulting curve in the ski will be greater. You finish your turns by following this curve in the pressured ski. The greater the side-cut and the greater the flexibility of the ski, the sharper will be the arc in which the ski can carve a turn. It is these features of the parabolic ski that make turning easier.

Length and Width: Other properties of a ski are its length and width. The longer ski will have greater stability than the shorter ski. The determinants of the proper length of ski for you are your weight and how fast you like to ski. The more you weigh and the faster you ski, the longer will be the ski you need for stability. However, the longer the ski, the harder it is to turn. Therefore, when selecting the proper length of ski for you, it should be long enough to give you stability for the speeds you use, but no longer than necessary.

The width of a ski is another feature that affects skiing. Wider skis have more surface area than narrower skis. More surface area provides greater stability. By providing more surface area, the wider ski permits you to ski a shorter length ski. The disadvantage of width is that as the ski becomes wider, the ability to set the ski on edge becomes more difficult.

Torsion: The longitudinal flexibility of a ski tip is its torsion. Torsion permits the tip of a ski to bend when the edge of the tip runs into a bump, explaining why torsion is highly desirable in moguls.

Choosing the right ski

How then does one select the right ski? Dialing in the factors of flexibility, side-cut, length and width sounds very complicated.When first learning to ski, you will ski with caution, going slowly and finding turning difficult. Therefore, as a novice, you should start with short, flexible skis with moderate side-cut and short length. As you become more proficient, you will find yourself skiing faster and your skis wiggling or chattering as you go. This is the time to get longer skis with other features. There is no magic formula that fits all skiers. The better skier you are, the more you will appreciate the subtleties of these factors. The best way to chose a ski is by trial and error. When you can, it is best to rent a pair of skis before you buy them. What feels right for your friend may not be quite right for you.

The terrain and type of snow you ski on is another factor in choosing a ski. Hard-pack snow, moguls, and deep powder each have different requirements. On hard-pack a stiffer ski performs better than a flexible ski; in moguls a ski with a soft tip is important; and in deep powder, a very flexible, wider, and shorter ski will give the best performance. Thus, no single ski is ideal in all conditions. For this reason, many skiers own more than one pair of skis and on a given day will select the one that seems best for the snow conditions of that day. One more point to note in selecting the right ski for you is that using your height as a guideline for ski length is an old rule of thumb that should be disregarded.

The 4 basic skills

The goal in skiing is to control the skis under your feet; and there are only 4 things you can do to skis:

1. Set them on edge
2. Distribute your weight between the front and back of the skis as well as between the two skis
3. Rotate or pivot them
4. Increase or decrease the pressure on them

These 4 skills, **edging, balancing, rotating, and**

pressure control, are the only skills used in skiing. Beginner, intermediate, and expert skiers all use the same 4 basic skills; the primary difference is in the way they use them. The beginner usually starts with just edging and balancing in their simplest forms and will depend on shoulder rotation to turn. The intermediate will edge and balance in more than one way and may add unweighting or pressure release in some form. The expert skier will use all 4 skills in a variety of ways depending upon the slope and snow conditions and will combine these skills with precise timing and subtle energy saving actions to achieve the picture of grace and elegance.

In the late 1970's, the Manual of the Professional Ski Instructors Association (PSIA) described only three basic skills in skiing: **Edging, rotating, and pressure control**. Since then, the PSIA manual has changed; balancing has been separated from pressure. PSIA now speaks of four movements: Edging, balancing, rotating, and pressure control movements. Pressure on a ski refers to the amount of force on the ski. Increasing the pressure or force on a ski is accomplished by increasing the amount of weight on the ski and/or by extending the knee. Pressure on the ski is released by jumping up or by flexing your knee.

Gentle versus steep slopes

The steepness of a slope is one of the main factors that determines the type of turns required to descend it. On gentle slopes, many different types of turns are effective; easy methods work as well as hard ones. However, on steep slopes, only the more difficult types of turns are practical as the easier ones result in skiing too fast.

Safety

While the first objective in skiing may be to get down the hill, the second objective, to get down safely, is by far more important. Safety in skiing means speed control, an accomplishment achieved by turning and braking. While all four skills are involved in speed control, the most important action is controlling your edges with your knees.

Recreational versus racing skiing

Skiing owes much of its development as a refined sport to ski racers. In their search for faster speeds, racers have discovered different and better ways to edge, balance, rotate, and alter pressure on the skis. They have found the best ways to make turns that minimize the loss of speed and maximize efficiency of movement. The technics they use on the racing courses are designed for top speed with good control. However, it is also known that a fall at high speed can do more body damage than a fall at slow speed. Because of this, recreational skiers are taught that controlling speed is more important than attaining speed; that turns are used to reduce speed or maintain a reasonable speed; and that safety, not speed, is the goal of recreational skiing.

These different objectives, speed for the racer and safety for the recreational skier, result in very different styles of skiing. While the recreational and racing skier use the same basic skills, they often use them in different ways for different purposes. For maximum speed through a turn, racers often perform stem turns by stepping from one ski to the other and applying all of their weight (and pressure) to the turning ski. This produces the maximum curve in the ski to achieve the sharpest turn possible, on the edge of the ski, by carving while minimizing skidding. Skidding, a sideways movement of the ski, reduces speed and loses races.

It must be appreciated that the racer's step turn is a type of stem turn; it is but one method of initiating turns and is used in situations where maintaining high speed is desired. On steep slopes, speed control can only be achieved by unweighting both feet simultaneously and quickly rotating them from one side of the fall line to the other. The turn is completed by carving or skidding. Further speed control is obtained by checking: rolling the edges of the skis into the hill to intentionally produce a short skid.

Racers try to avoid the technics that reduce speed just as recreational skiers try to develop them. Therefore, recreational skiers should not regard all the technics used by racers as the "best" way to ski. Recreational skiers should apply racing technics only when appropriate and realize that it is the two-legged parallel turn that is most useful on difficult terrain. There is a place in skiing for both one and two-legged turns. The advanced skier will learn them both and use each of them where needed.

Chapter 2

Anatomy of a turn

A. Initiation of a turn
1. Edge change
2. Stem turns
3. Parallel turns pivoting
B. Completion of a turn
1. Skidding
2. Carving

Summary: Turns are initiated by changing the direction of the skis by either an edge change or a pivot. Edge change transfers weight from one set of edges to the other. This is done by transferring weight from one ski to the inside edge of the other or by flattening and pivoting the two skis together.

Turns are completed by either skidding or carving. Skidding is the combination of sideslipping with rotation of the tails of the skis around the tips. Carving is following the direction the ski tips are pointing. In carving there is no sideslipping and no rotation.

Initiating a Turn

Initiating a turn is the first step in changing the direction of the skis. Once the direction starts to change, the completion phase begins. Turns are initiated either by an edge change, stemming one ski, or a pivot of both feet together.

Edge change is accomplished on either one or two legs. The one legged change is a stem turn or weight transfer. The two legged change is a knee or hip roll, or a pivot of both feet after a moment of pressure release.

Stem turns are turns initiated by pointing one ski in the new direction, setting it on its inside edge, and then transferring the body's weight to that ski. The weight shift is from one foot to the other so that there is always

Figure 3 **Stem Turn**

A stem turn is a one-legged turn performed by transferring the body's weight to one leg. Skiing downhill, the heel is pushed outward and the knee angulated inward to place the stemmed ski on its inside edge, facing in the new direction. Then the hips shift their weight to the stemmed ski. Simultaneous pressure release from both feet is unnecessary in stem turns.

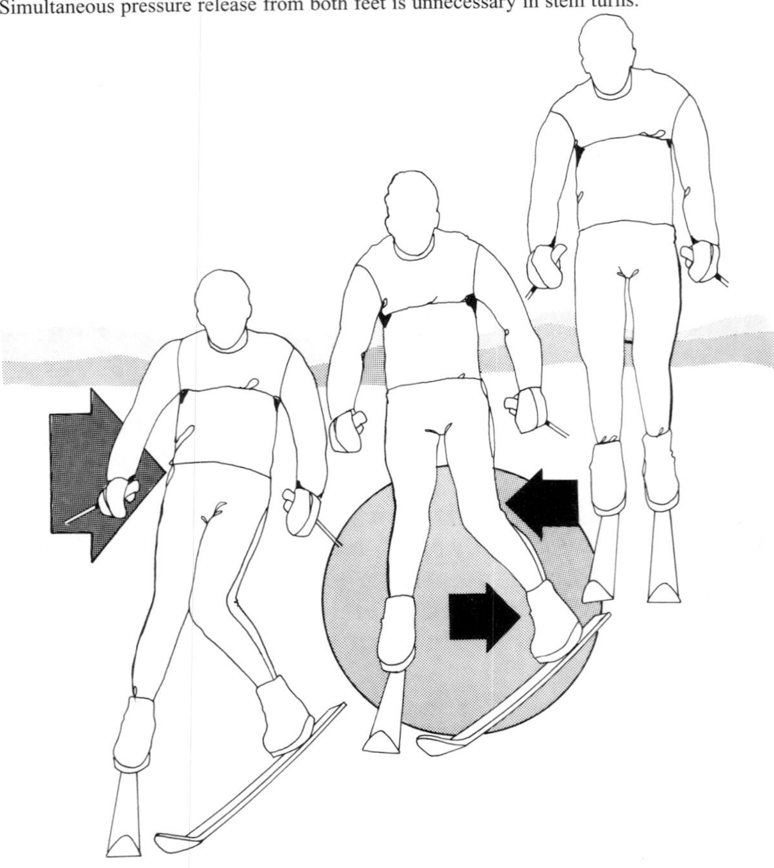

some weight on the ground **[Figure 3]**. The stem turn is a one legged turn in which almost all weight is transferred to the stemmed ski. Only a minimal amount remains on the other ski. Stem turns can be accomplished at very slow speeds but work better with some speed for momentum.

Parallel turns by edge change can be initiated by a one legged or two legged move. The one legged move is

Edge Change

Figure 4

Edge change can initiate a parallel turn. By rolling the knees from one side to the other, the edges of the skis will change, as will the direction of the arc in the skis.

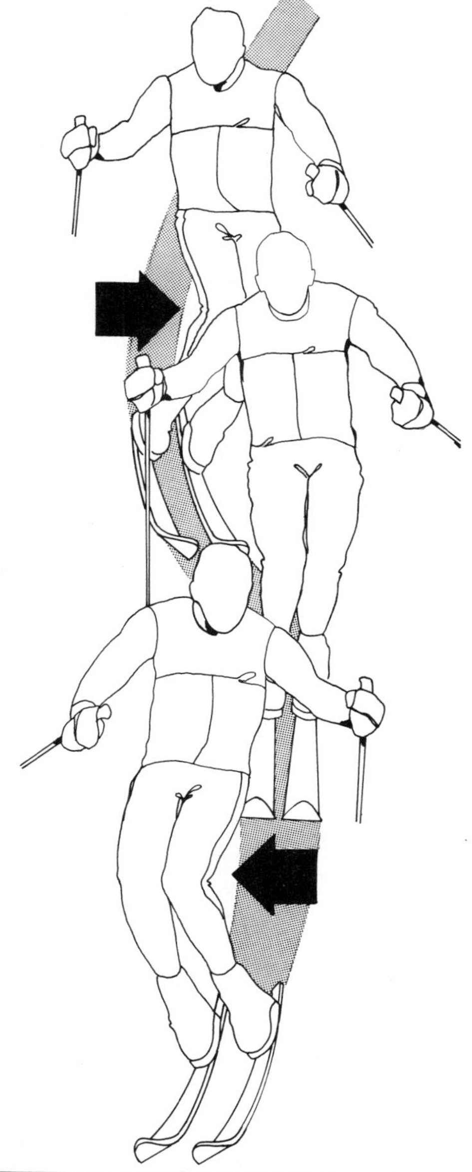

performed by weight transfer from one ski to the other and requires some speed to provide momentum to turn. The turn is initiated by first placing all weight on the downhill ski which usually involves flexing the down hill ski a little more. To emphasize this when learning, you can lift the heel of the uphill ski as you balance completely on the downhill ski, and tip the uphill ski on its outside edge. The turn begins by extending (straightening) the knee of the uphill leg, which will transfer weight from the downhill to the uphill ski. This action will simultaneously roll the uphill ski onto its inside edge to maintain balance. This type of edge change is a weight transfer and does not require a moment of simultaneous pressure release of both skis.

Figure 5 **Foot twist**

Rotation is used to initiate a parallel turn. While the feet, hips, or shoulders can rotate in the direction of the turn, it is best to rotate just the feet ("foot twist" or "foot swivel"), rather than the upper body. If pressure is released just prior to rotation, foot twist is much easier to perform.

Edge change by both feet simultaneously can be accomplished by rolling the flexed knees form one side to the other (knee crossovers) **[Figure 4]** or by moving the hips and upper body from one side to the other (hip crossovers). This can be performed without altering the pressure on the skis, as discussed in the Chapter 10: Smooth Slopes. It can also be facilitated by a moment of weightlessness on both feet by pressure release. (The older term for this is unweighting). It is accomplished in one of a few ways as discussed in Chapter 7: Pressure Control. The simplest way is to quickly hop upwards, but it can also be achieved by a quick bend of the knees to drop the seat downwards or by a quick lift of the heels beneath the seat called leg retraction.

Parallel turns by pivoting or rotating both skis together is the other way of initiating a turn. This requires a moment of pressure release of both feet simultaneously. At the moment of pressure release, both feet twist in the direction of the turn **[Figure 5]**. The rotation can be achieved by twisting the feet, hips, or shoulders in the direction of the turn, although twisting the feet is the simplest and most frequently used technic.

When initiating parallel turns with pressure release, weight is often transferred from one foot to the other, although this is not necessary. Weight can remain on both feet throughout the turn as is often done in deep powder.

Completing a Turn

Once the direction of the skis has changed, the completion phase of the turning action commences. Turns are completed by following either the arc of a curved ski (carving) or the side of the ski (skidding). Both actions use the same basic mechanism: edgeset. The difference between the two is the degree of edgeset and the distribution of weight between the tips and tails of the skis.

With the skis barely on edge, skidding with sideways movement results; with an increase in degree of edging, sideways movement is checked and the skis move forward, following the arc in the edged ski, carving. In practice, most turns finish with some element of both carving and skidding.

Figure 6 **Sideslipping**

Sideslipping is moving downhill with the side of the ski leading the way. The edges of the skis are partially flattened against the slope to initiate sliding down the hill. The slide is checked (stopped) by increasing the degree of edgeset into the hill. The prime movers of the skis' edges are the knees. The knees roll downhill to begin sideslipping and roll uphill to check it.

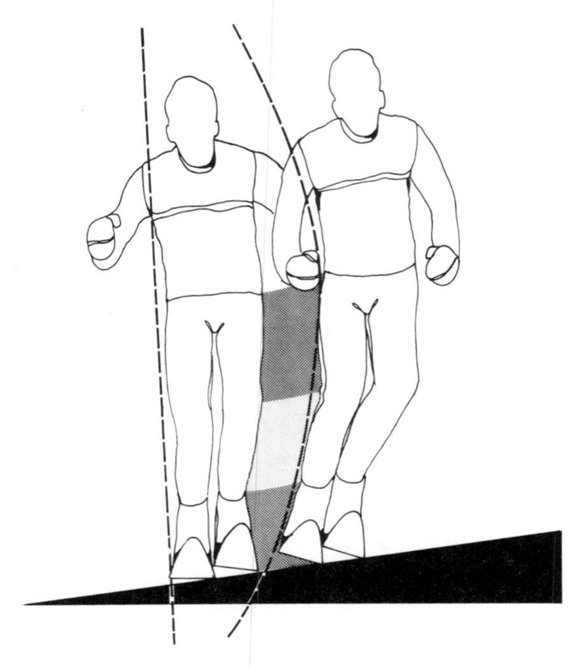

An understanding of carving and skidding begins with sideslipping. Sideslipping is moving sideways down a slope with the skis perpendicular to the fall line and the tips and tails of the skis moving at the same speed. Sideslipping is controlled by movement of the flexed knees toward and away from the hill **[Figure 6]**.

Skidding is the combination of sideslipping plus rotation of the tails of the skis around the tips because the tails are slipping faster than the tips **[Figure 7]**. This is accomplished by transferring weight forward, by pushing the shins against your boot tops and feeling more weight on the balls of your feet. The amount of forward lean adjusts the arc of the skidded turn. Short radius or sharp

Skidding *Figure 7*

Skidding is sideslipping combined with rotation of the tails of the skis around the tips. The path is shown here. The side of the ski leads the way through the turn. Skidding is produced by enough flattening of the edges of the skis to permit sideslipping and leaning forward so more weight is on the ski tips than the tails.

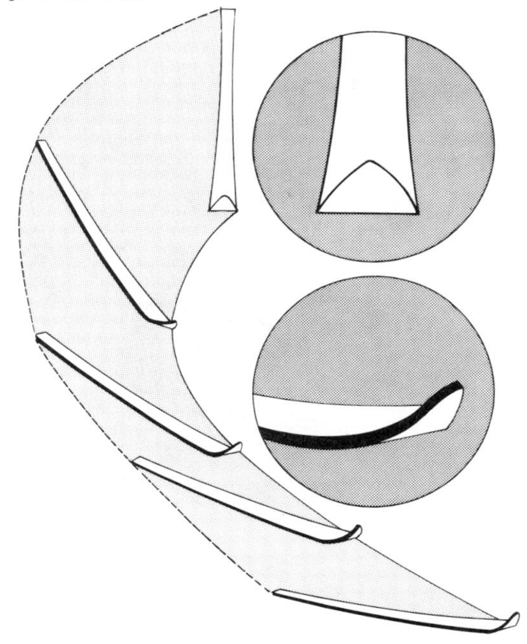

turns, with a small arc, are made by transferring considerable weight forward, whereas long radius or gradual turns with wider arcs, are performed with less forward lean. The more weight remaining on the heels during a skidded turn, the slower the turn and the more gradual the arc.

It is difficult, and sometimes impossible, to skid in deep powder because the snow offers too much resistance to sideslipping. For this reason, skidded turns are generally limited to hard-packed or shallow powder slopes. Indeed, the most common reason for having trouble skiing in deep powder is trying to finish turns by skidding. Skidding is effective in powder only when it is light and not too deep (See Chapter 10: Powder). The solution to

Figure 8 **Carving**

Carving is following the direction the skis are pointing. Carving is produced by edging the skis far enough to prevent sideslipping. The tips of the skis lead the way through a carved turn. Both the tips and tails must bear some weight when carving.

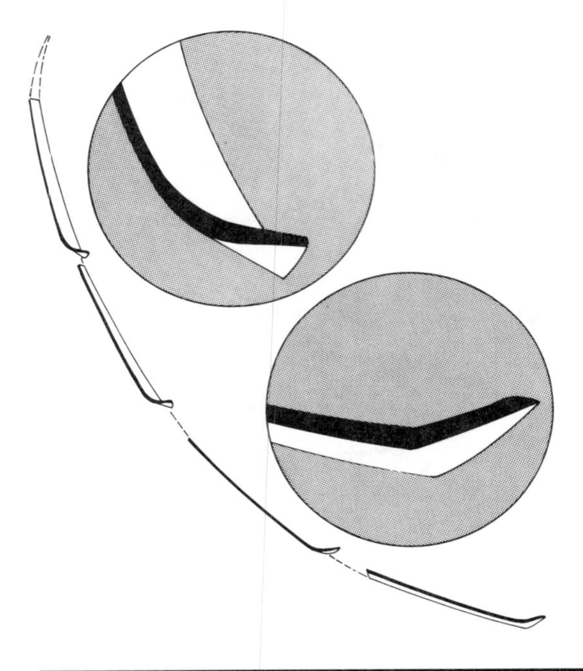

turning in deep powder is carving.

Carving is traveling in the direction the skis are pointing without sideslipping. When the skis are edged, the line of the skis' direction will be curved due to the reversed camber in the skis that is produced by your body weight and the flexibility of the skis. Therefore, the carved turn is one that follows the arc of the edged ski **[Figure 8]**. The carved turn can be initiated by either an edge change or a pivot. Carving refers to the completion phase of the turn.

Carving differs from skidding in two ways. First, carving requires a greater degree of edging than skidding. To skid, the edges must lie flat enough against the hill to **permit** slipping; to carve, the edgeset must increase

Skidding initiated by edge change or foot twist *Figure 9*

A turn completed by skidding can begin with edge change or foot twist. Edge change is a smoother, gentler initiation, while foot twist produces a sharper turn with a smaller radius.

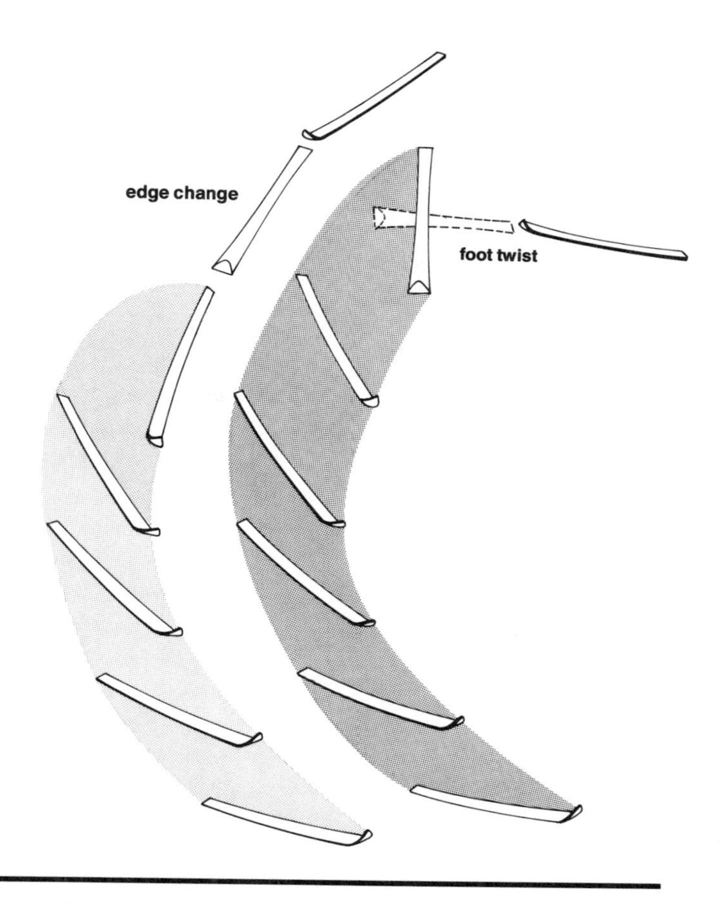

enough to **prevent** skidding. Second, in skidding, the skis change direction by rotating the tails around the tips. In carving, there is no rotation; the tails do not rotate around the tips.

Technically, all combinations of initiating and completing turns are possible. A turn completed by skidding can be initiated by an edge change or a foot twist

Figure 10 **Carving initiated by edge change or foot twist**

A carved turn may begin with edge change or foot twist. Edge change followed by carving produces the "pure" carved turn. It is a gradual, gentle turn. Initiating a turn by foot twist and completing it by carving produces a quicker, sharper turn.

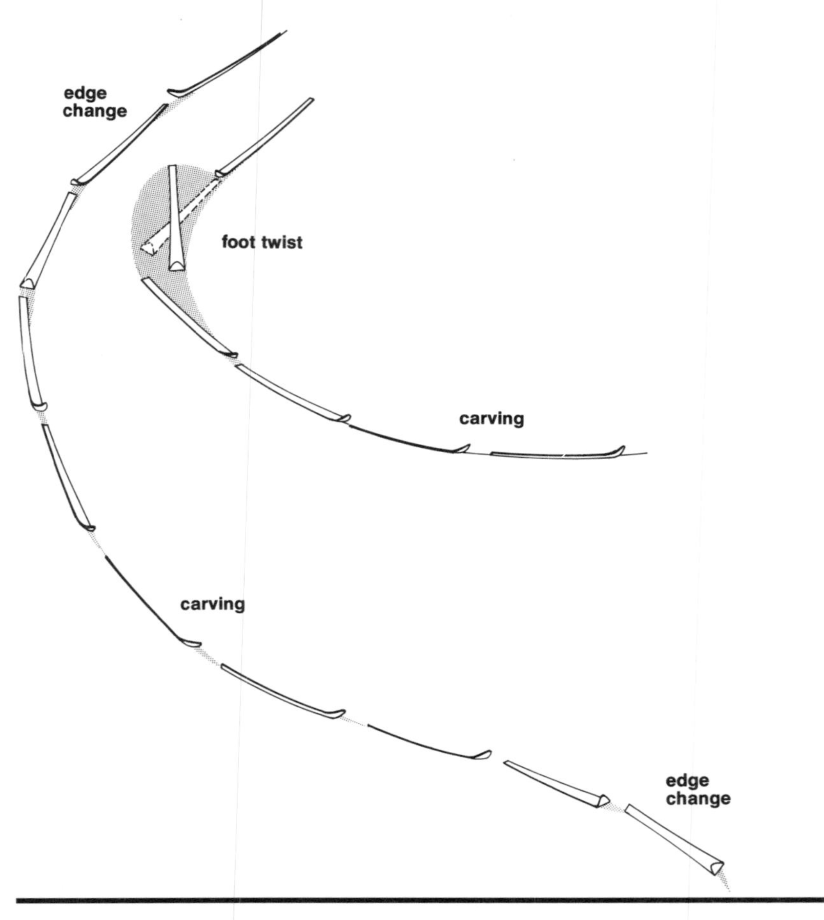

[Figure 9]. Similarly, carved turns may be initiated by an edge change or a foot twist. Edge changing and carving produce the smooth, graceful turn that may be described as the "pure" carved turn. By combining foot rotation with carving a sharper turn results **[Figure 10]**.

In practice, most turns finish with some element of both carving and skidding. While carving is the better and more controlled way of completing turns, it is usually difficult to avoid some degree of skidding in most turns.

Knee angulation is the primary action that will stop a skid and convert it to a carve. In many situations, straight knees prevent enough edging to carve, so that the skis simply sideslip and skid downhill. Flexing the knees permit them to angulate, thereby increasing their degree of edging and permitting them to hold the snow to stop sideslipping and skidding. If you are having trouble carving on steep slopes, check your knees for enough flexion and knee angulation. (See Chapter 4: Edging)

Chapter 3

Knees and Shoulders–an Overview

Shoulder Rotation
No shoulder rotation (Anticipation)
Knee Angulation--knee flexion
Pressure Release
Banking and hip angulation

Summary: Three important skills are necessary to progress from intermediate to advanced skiing:

1. **Shoulder rotation--using the turning power of shoulder rotation without rotating your shoulders**
2. **Knee angulation--for edge control to regulate speed**
3. **Pressure release---removing weight from both feet simultaneously to permit pivoting of the skis and quick turns**

Hip angulation and banking (or inward lean) are two more skills which should be added but are not as vital as these three.

The next five chapters describe in detail how to perform each of these skills. This chapter discusses why you should focus on these skills and the principles behind them.

Shoulder rotation

Watching a baseball player swing a bat, you notice the momentum of the bat rotates the arms around the batter's body. Not only do the arms rotate, but the shoulders, hips, and eventually the legs all rotate in the same direction. Even the back foot pivots at the end of the swing. This illustrates the turning forces generated by simply rotating the arms and shoulders; the rotational force is quickly transferred to the lower half of the body.

When first learning to ski, you probably discovered that one of the most instinctive ways to turn is to rotate your shoulders as if you are turning the steering wheel of a car. If you turn your shoulders hard to one side, your lower body will eventually follow in the same direction, as will your skis. This works by the same mechanism that turns the baseball player's legs. The long muscles of the abdomen and spine are twisted and stretched when your shoulders rotate. The stretched muscles try to shorten and untwist as soon as possible. They will therefore pull the lower body to face in the same direction as the upper body as long as the position of the upper body is fixed in the new direction

The rotational power that turning the shoulders geer-ates can be used in two ways: rotating your shoulders as you turn or rotating them before you turn. Intermediate skiers usually rotate their shoulders as they turn, initiating the turn with shoulder rotation and completing the turn by "following through" with the outside arm, another form of shoulder rotation. By this maneuver, the shoulders remain facing in the same direction as the ski tips. The next turn is performed by rotating the shoulders in the opposite direction.

No shoulder rotation–Anticipation

Better skiers have their shoulders rotated before the turn. Notice I said "have their shoulders rotated" rather than "rotate their shoulders". The difference is important. Better skiers try to keep their shoulders facing downhill all the time, while their legs and skis rhythmically turn from one side to the other. The shoulders don't actively rotate; they stay in the same position constantly, facing down the fall line. Only the lower body rotates from one side to the other. As a result, before each turn, the shoulders are in a rotated position compared to the lower body, even though the shoulders haven't rotated. And, it is this **twisted (or torqued) position of the shoulders in relation to the legs that supplies the main force to** pivot the skis from one direction to another.

When your shoulders face in one direction and the skis in another, the rotation force is present. If while traversing a hill you twist your shoulders so that your upper body faces straight downhill and then you quickly release pressure from your feet (by going "down-UP", for example), in that moment of "weightlessness" your feet and skis will pivot to face where your shoulders are facing (downhill). Rotating your shoulders to face downhill is called **anticipation*** because the shoulders anticipate the new direction the skis are about to acquire.

This is similar to twisting a thick rubber band which

Anticipation *Figure 11*

Anticipation is turning the head, shoulders, and arms downhill before the feet turn. This stretches the long abdominal and back muscles. At the moment of pressure release, the stretched muscles shorten, pulling the feet around automatically to face in the same direction as the upper body.

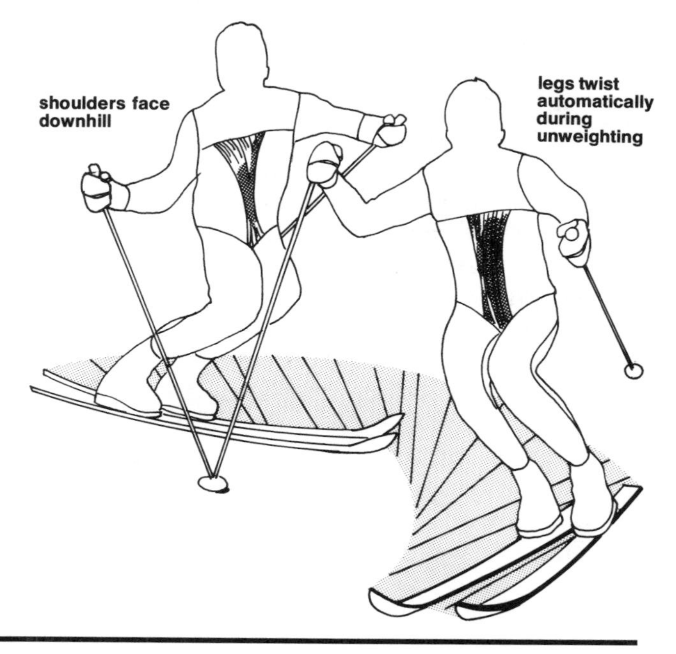

is held vertically between the thumb and index finger of each hand. When the upper end of the rubber band is rotated 90° in one direction while the lower end remains fixed, the rubber band is twisted and tight.When you release the lower end, the rubber band straightens by the lower end untwisting so it faces in the same direction as the upper end.

* *First described by the French ski expert, Georges Joubert*

Your body has many vertical running muscles along your spine and abdomen which can be compared to the vertically held rubber band. When you stand with your feet in place and twist your shoulders to face a new direction, these muscles are stretched and twisted. If you hold your shoulders in this new direction, the stretched body muscles will try to straighten. As they do, they will rotate your lower body so it faces in the same direction as your upper body. This rotational force eventually reaches your feet and results in rotating your skis to face in the new direction, unless friction and your weight on the skis prevent the skis from rotating. It is to permit rotation to occur that the pressure on the skis must be released by some form of pressure release. This is similar to what happened to the lower end of the rubber band when it was released **[Figure 11]**.

Note that the rotational power to turn is present when the upper body is twisted to face downhill. However, nothing happens until the feet are released, just as the rubber band remains twisted with stored energy until the lower end is released.

Advanced skiers seldom traverse between turns; the completion of one turn is the beginning of the next. Good skiers try to hold their shoulders facing downhill **all the time**, not rotating them with each turn, so they are **always** anticipating the next turn. You can see this demonstrated by studying the tracks left in powder snow by good skiers and not so good skiers.

However, don't focus attention on maintaining your shoulders facing downhill until you have acquired two other skills: Knee angulation and pressure release. The order for learning is:

1. learn knee angulation, to control your turns and speed with your knees **alone**
2. learn pressure release with a down-UP motion, to take the weight off both feet **simultaneously**, to let you begin turns with a quick pivot.
3. After learning these, you're ready to concentrate on keeping your shoulders facing downhill.

In order to hold your shoulders facing downhill all the time, you must be able to control your speed and your turns without employing shoulder rotation during the turn. Intermediate skiers usually rotate their shoulders through each turn because they haven't developed other braking skills.

The answer to freeing up your shoulders so they can constantly face downhill and not rotate through each turn is to use the ski edges to control your turns and your speed instead of your shoulders. And, the edges are controlled primarily by your knees. **Knee angulation** is the action that best controls the ski's edges. Hip angulation can also play a role, as can banking, but concentrate on knee angulation first. The others can be added later. (Shoulder rotation, and non-rotation, are discussed further in Chapter 8: Rotation).

Knee angulation–knee flexion

Knee angulation is the first, and most important, skill to acquire in learning to be a better skier. Once you can control your skis with your knees, you free your shoulders for "constant anticipation" which will make turning easier and quicker. Until you can control your turns with your knees, forget about keeping your shouders facing downhill all the time because you will need your shoulders for survival (as you have probably learned).

Knee angulation is rolling your knees to the side to set your skis on their edges. To perform knee angulation, you must first bend (or flex) your knees. Knee bending thus becomes the first requirement for good skiing. Because of the way the knee is constructed, you cannot roll your knees to the side when the knees are straight; they must be flexed. And, the more they are flexed, the greater the degree of knee angulation that is attainable.

This is very important. To achieve good edge control, you must angulate your knees; to angulate your knees you must first flex them. To improve your skiing, knee flexion and knee angulation is the place to begin. Once you can control your edges with your knees, you can progress. (Knee Angulation is discussed in Chapter 4: Edging methods).

Pressure release

On shallow pitches a variety of technics which do not require unweighting can work well. However, controlling your speed on steep pitches requires short radius turns, quick turns, turns that rapidly change the direction of your skis. This can only be achieved by pivoting both skis in unison at the beginning of the turn.

Transferring weight from one ski to the other won't do; the turn is not fast enough. Only a quick pivot provides a rapid, controlled turn; and you must have a moment of weightlessness on both feet to permit your skis to pivot.

Standing still, if you rotate your shoulders quickly to one side your skis may rotate a little in the same direction, but not very far; friction and your weight will try to keep them in their tracks. However, if you momentarily take the weight off your feet just as you rotate your shoulders, your skis will quickly pivot to follow your upper body. This moment of weightlessness is called unweighting, or **pressure release**.

Pressure release is one of the toughest stumbling blocks for intermediate skiers. Many intermediates go down-UP, but then very quickly step or transfer their weight from one foot to the other thinking they are doing it correctly. Alas, they are not. Perhaps fear of losing contact with the ground is playing a role. If so, this fear must be conquered to become a better skier; there is no substitute for proper pressure release.

Technology in ski design continues to introduce equipment that makes skiing easier than it was in earlier years. Modern skis respond easily and quickly to gentle movements of the body. As a result, turns on easy slopes can often be performed with subtle weight shifts and just a little flexion/extension movement of the legs; pressure release is seldom needed. However, under difficult slope conditions (moguls, steep slopes, deep powder, crud) pressure release is still necessary. Therefore, if you hope to ski steep or bumpy slopes, you will have to learn to release pressure.

There are several ways to release pressure and advanced skiers will often use different technics of unweighting in the same run. However, the principle of pressure release, to provide a weightless moment in which to pivot your skis, remains the same regardless of which method you use. (See Chapter 7: Pressure Control).

Banking and hip angulation

Banking and hip angulation are the two other forms of edging besides knee angulation. While these must also be learned to ski well, they are easier to learn than knee angulation. Learn knee angulation as soon as possible. It gives you delicate edge control and is sometimes the only means of edge control when moving slowly. (See Chapter 4: Edging).

Chapter 4
Edging

Knee angulation
Knee flexion(bending)
Hip angulation
Banking

Summary: Edge control, or controlling the edges of the skis, is the first principle of skiing. Edge control can be achieved in different ways, but the most important is by combining two actions of the knees: Flexion (bending the knees) and angulation (pushing the knees to the side). Knee angulation is the main action that controls the edges. However, knee angulation is only possible when the knees are flexed. The two other means of edging are hip angulation and banking.

As mentioned in Chapter 1, the primary difference between a ski and a flat board is that a ski has sharp edges. The edges of a ski are its most important element because it is the edges that control your speed and permit you to stop. If you place a ski flat on a hill, it will slide down hill, out of control, just as a flat board would slide. However, if you press the edge of that ski into the hill, the ski will stop. Therefore, most skiing is done on the edges of the skis, rather than the flat bottoms, and many of the body movements on skis are aimed at controlling the ski's edges.

The edges of the skis are controlled by movements of the legs. This occurs because the ski is firmly attached to the boot and the boot is fit snugly to the foot. Therefore movements of the legs are transmitted directly to the ski. This is the reason for a tight-fitting ski boot. When you move your legs and knees you want the ski to move immediately and appropriately. This cannot be done if your foot is loose in your boot. Rolling your knees together puts the skis on their inside edges; rolling the knees apart

Figure 12 **Inside and outside edges**

The inside and outside edges of the skis are controlled by lateral (sideways) movements of the knees. On the left, the skis are set on their inside edges by rolling the knees inward to touch each other. On the right, the skis are set on their outside edges by rolling the knees away from each other. In both actions, there is no ankle motion because the stiff boots prevent it.

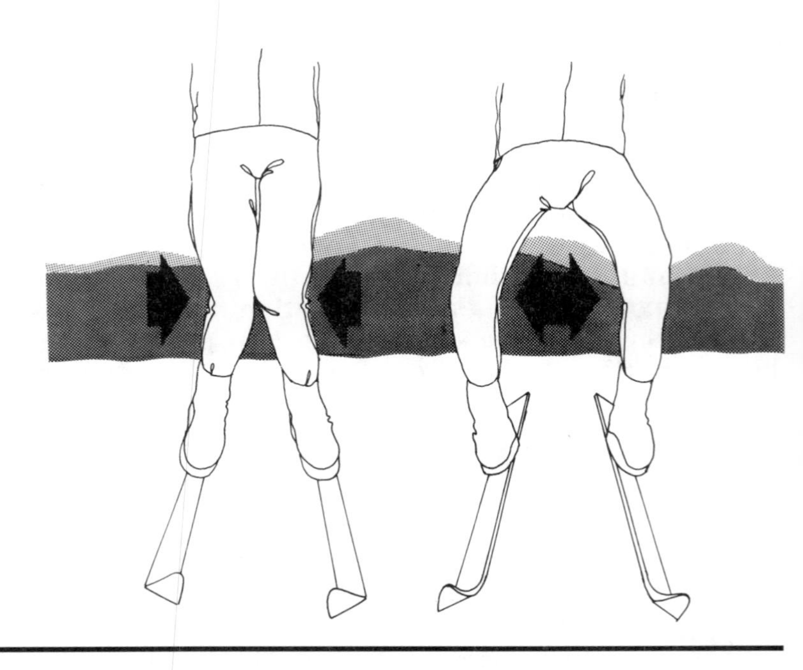

puts them on their outside edges **[Figure 12]**.

Theoretically, three joints have the ability to produce an edge change: the ankle, knee, and hip. The ankle plays no role because the stiff, tight ski boot prevents sideways (or lateral) movements of the ankle. The other two joints, the knee and hip, work together to control the ski edges.

Knee Angulation

Knee angulation is rolling your knees to the side to set the skis on their inside edges. Knee angulations requires that your knee joints be bent (flexed) because knee angulation cannot be performed with extended legs and a straight knee joint. Knee angulation is made possible by combined actions of the hip and knee joints. The hip joint is a ball-and-socket joint and as such is capable of movements in all directions. However, the effect of the hips on the ski edges depends on whether the knees are extended (straight) or flexed (bent). When the knees are extended, the knee joints are locked and rigid, thus unable to contribute any assistance in edging the skis; only the hip joints can move, and the hips' effect on the ski edges is limited. On the other hand, when the knees are flexed the knee joints are unlocked. The hips can now roll the knees in one direction, which automatically rolls the skis onto their edges.

Wedge with straight and flexed knees *Figure 13*

A) The wedge (or snow plow) position with the thighs pushed apart, the toes turned inward, and the heels pushed outward. The knees are straight and the skis lie slightly on their inside edges. **B)** The same position as A with one exception: The knees and ankles are now flexed, permitting the knees to roll inward, almost touching each other. The result is a significant increase in the degree of edgeset by the inside edges of the skis.

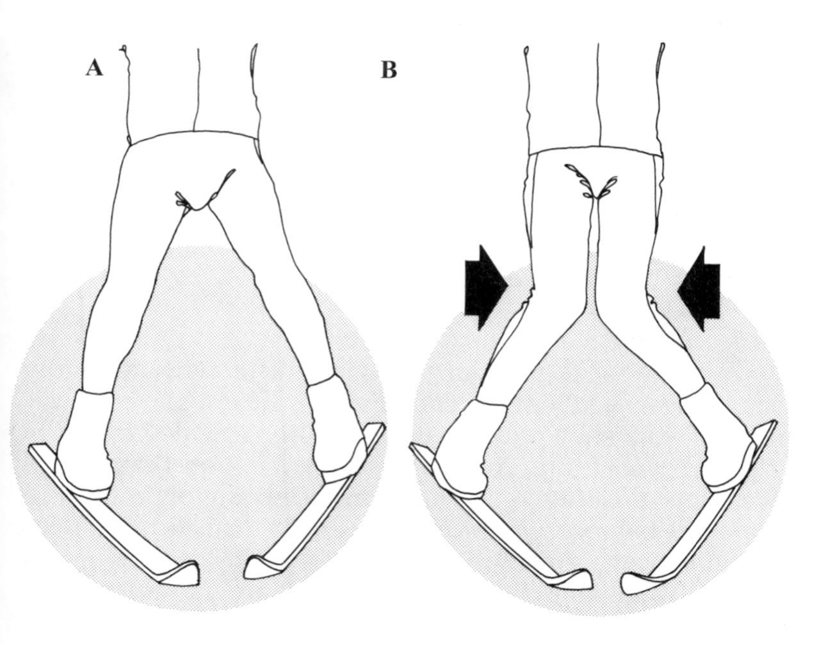

Knee Flexion

The old expression from European ski schools, "Bend zee knees five dollars please," is just as true today as it was generations ago. Bending your knees is an essential action in skiing. For those who think that you can learn to ski with straight knees–forget it. It won't work! The anatomy of your body, and specifically your legs, will limit your ability to control your edges if your knees are extended. Flexing your knees permits your knees to roll sideways (knee angulation) thereby edging your skis. And the more you flex your knees, the greater will be the degree of knee angulation achievable.

To better understand how the knee and hip joints work together, **Figures 13 and 14** illustrate the difference in degree of edge set with extended and flexed knees. In the snowplow position with extended knees, your hips set the skis on their inside edges by rotating the toes inward and the heels outward **[Figure 13A]**. While the skis are on their inside edges, the degree of edging is limited. On gentle slopes, this degree of edging with extended knees may be effective in speed control, but on steep slopes a greater degree of edging is required. By flexing your knees while still in the snowplow position, the knees can move towards each other, almost touching. (The actual motion is internal hip rotation.) This increases the degree of inside edging which provides greater braking power. Note that pushing the heels further apart will increase the degree of edging even more **[Figure 13B]**.

Hip Angulation

With the skis parallel, the same difference in edging can be observed with extended versus flexed knees as was noted in the snowplow position. With extended knees in a parallel position, your hips set the skis on their uphill edges by pushing the hips uphill (hip angulation). To maintain balance, your shoulders must lean in the opposite direction, downhill **[Figure 14A]**. The amount of edging obtainable by hip angulation alone is limited. On steep slopes, edging with hip angulation and extended knees is often inadequate. But by flexing the knees, the knees can be rolled sideways resulting in knee angulation

Hip and knee angulation *Figure 14*

A.) Hip angulation alone. The hips push uphill and the shoulders drop downhill to set the skis on their uphill edges. The knees are straight. The amount of edging obtainable is limited. **B). Hip and knee angulation**. Flexing (bending) the knees unlocks the knee joints making it possible for the knees to be pushed sideways (knee angulation), along with the hips. The addition of knee angulation permits a much greater degree of edging than hip angulation alone. This has been called the "comma position" because the body configuration is curved like a comma. **C.) Knee angulation alone.** The hips and shoulders remain straight. The degree of edging attainable with knee angulation alone is close to that in "B" where both hip and knee angulation are combined.

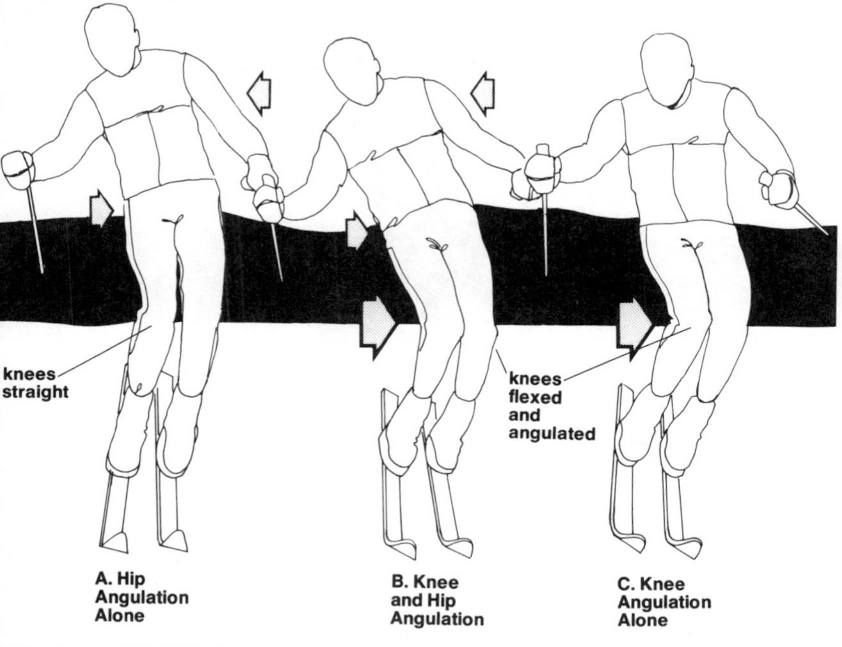

and allowing the skis to roll further onto their edges. **Figure 14B** illustrates combined hip and knee angulation. This is the "comma position" of older ski schools.

In everyday skiing, knee angulation is much more important than hip angulation, particularly when linking short turns. Further, the addition of hip angulation adds very little additional edging to knee angulation alone. Good skiing emphasizes a quiet upper body, with the edges controlled primarily by the knees **[Figure 14C]**. Hip angulation is usually not needed and is to be avoided

Figure 15 **Knee angulation**

The skis are rolled high on their right edges by knee angulation, rolling the knees to the right. Note that the knees are considerably flexed in order to permit this degree of knee angulation. (Copper Mountain photo by Rick Godin.)

because it is much faster to roll the knees from side to side than to roll the hips in one direction, the shoulders in the opposite direction, and then reverse these positions with every turn. Knee angulation can increase edge setting without displacing the body's center of gravity **[Figures 14C and 15]**. Although hip angulation assists in edge control, knee angulation does most of the work.

Flexing your knees **all the time** is a good idea. This permits you to be prepared to angulate them at a moment's notice. As you ride up a chair lift, note the good skiers below you. They will usually have their knees flexed throughout every turn. From the flexed-knee position, they may flex their knees further or partially extend them, but they rarely straighten them completely. The degree of knee flexion is dynamic, constantly changing, much like the shock absorbers in your car.

Banking

Banking is the third method of edging, the other two methods being knee and hip angulation as just described. Banking sets your skis on edge by leaning your entire body inward, towards the center of a turn. If you make a right turn while skiing with some speed, the body will feel a force pulling it in the opposite direction, to the left. This force, which always pulls away from the center of the turn, is called centrifugal force. To counteract centri**fugal** force the entire body can lean to the right in the direction of the turn. This transfers weight and pressure to the ski edges and results in applying a counterforce to the centrifugal force. (Leaning inward towards the center of a turn is applying centri**petal** force). The faster your speed while turning, the greater the centrifugal force to pull you away from the turn, the greater the pressure on your edges as you lean inward, and the greater will be the angle at which the body can lean inward to increase edge setting. At slow speeds there is less centrifugal force so the body cannot lean inward as far, therefore, less edging is possible.

Leaning in the direction of the turn is called banking. It is the same action used by a bicyclist or skater when making a turn at fast speeds. The cyclist and the skater also lean their bodies inward towards the center of the turn to counteract centrifugal force **[Figure 16]**.

Banking transfers weight to the edges of the skis. This results in edging, the same edging that is achieved by knee angulation or hip angulation. Good skiers use all of these methods for edge control, sometimes separately, at other times together **[Figure 17]**. Compared to knee angulation, banking uses less energy, requires more time, and must be corrected (by straightening up) when the turn is completed or when you slow down. Edging by knee angulation requires more work by the thigh muscles, but knee angulation provides faster edging, finer control, and

Figure 16 **Banking**

Banking is leaning inward toward the center of the turn to counteract centrifugal force. At higher speeds greater degrees of banking are possible. A skier banks just like a cyclist does.

easier adjustment of the ski edges. Hip angulation is the least important method of edging and seldom is used alone. Hip angulation is the secondary method of edge control; it supplements the primary forms, knee angulation and banking.

Banking has definite limitations. Banking, in combination with knee and hip angulation, will provide maximum edging and the quickest stopping. But as speed is reduced in stopping, the inward lean must be corrected to an upright position. Failing to straighten up soon enough results in falling uphill. This is a common cause for falling: too much uphill lean for too slow a speed.

Banking with knee angulation

Figure 17

Banking, performed by leaning the upper body inward, in the direction of the turn. In this photo, the skier is also angulating his knees and hips inward to increase the degree of edgeset. Note how high the skis are angulated. (Copper Mountain photo by Rick Godin).

Chapter 5
Edging: How to use it

Sideslipping and sidestepping
Stopping
Skidding and Carving
Wedge (Snowplow) and stem turns
Uphill and downhill stem
Edge control with the wedge
Garlands

Summary: Edging is used in many ways. Sideslipping, sidestepping, stopping, skidding, carving, snowplow turns, and stem turns all have in common their dependence on edge control. Knee flexion and knee angulation are the actions required.

Sideslipping and sidestepping

Sideslipping is one of the best ways to learn edge control. Sideslipping is moving sideways down a slope with the side of the skis leading the way. Sideslipping is controlled by movement of the flexed knees towards and away from the hill. These movements control the edges of the skis by setting them into the hill to slow down or stop and by flattening the edges against the slope to move sideways down the hill.

Sideslipping begins by standing still with the skis across the hill, perpendicular to the fall line. The knees should be flexed and angulated inward, towards the hill. The greater the degree of knee angulation uphill, the greater will be the degree of shoulder leaning downhill to maintain balance. The sideslip is started by gently rolling the knees away from the hill. As the knees roll away from the hill, balance is maintained by leaning the shoulders back uphill (See Figure 6, page 18). After the slide begins, it is controlled by rolling the knees back uphill to slow down. In sideslipping, the key movements are

Figure 18

Sideslipping, gentle vs. steep slope

In sideslipping, rolling the knees uphill to stop and downhill to slip is the key movement. The other parts of the body remain as quiet as possible. To begin slipping the degree of edging is decreased. On gentle slopes the skis may lie flat against the snow. On steep slopes the skis sideslip while still on their edges.

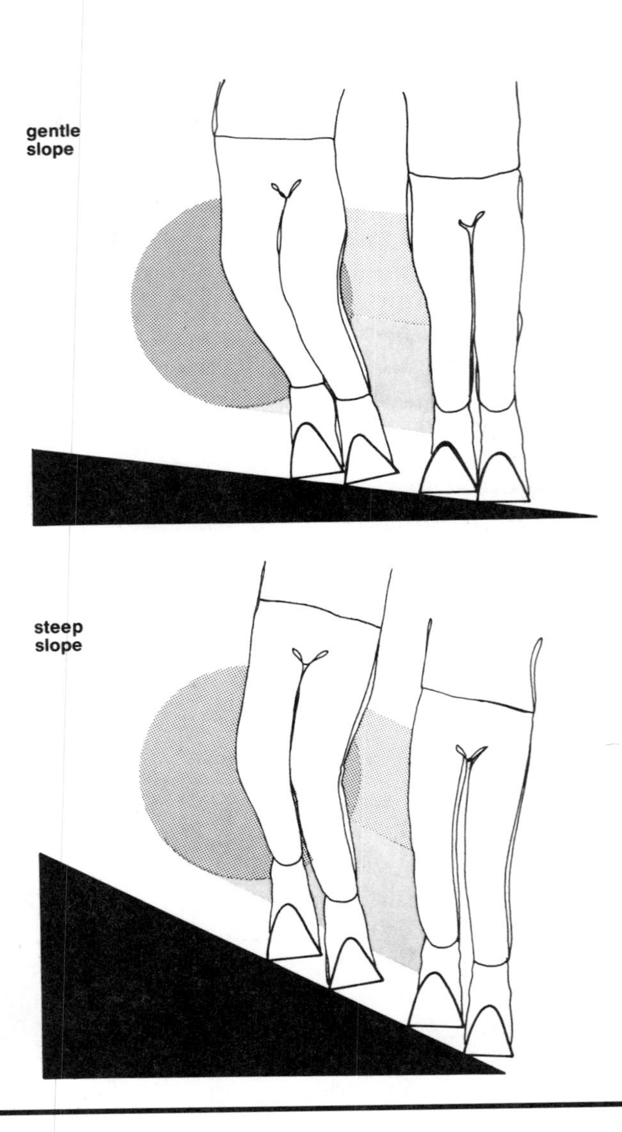

rolling the knees uphill to stop and downhill to start. Other than maintaining balance by compensatory movements of the shoulders down or uphill, in the opposite direction as the knees, the body, and especially the arms, should remain as quiet as possible.

Starting a sideslip may be difficult. You think "sideslip", but nothing happens. Sideslipping requires some steepness in the slope to be effective. On a very gentle slope, if the snow consistency is at all sticky, standing with the skis across the slope results in no side ways movement because the pull of gravity downhill cannot overcome the friction between skis and snow. Therefore, to practice sideslipping you should try it on a slope with moderate to steep pitch. The steeper the pitch, the easier it is to get started. Begin sideslipping by rolling the knees a little downhill. On steep slopes the skis begin to slide while they are still on their edges. On gentler slopes, the skis may lie almost flat against the snow before they start to move.

A common problem is failure of the uphill ski to slide with the downhill ski. This is caused by having too much weight on the uphill ski. When sideslipping, almost all of your weight should be on the downhill ski. One way to achieve this is by locking your knees together with the uphill ski a couple of inches ahead of the downhill ski. This way the uphill ski will move simultaneously with the downhill ski. For balance you want a little weight on the uphill ski, but very little. How much? This is only determined by trial and error with practice. **Figure 18** illustrates the difference in degree of knee angulation when sideslipping on gentle versus steeper slopes. On steep slopes, sideslipping begins while the knees are still angulated while on gentler slopes the knees are almost straight. However, remember that the knees must be flexed at all times to control the sideslip.

Sidestepping is walking up or downhill with the skis lying perpendicular, across the slope. In sidestepping uphill, the uphill ski plays an important role. The uphill ski leads the way by a sideways movement uphill while your weight is all on your downhill ski. Once the uphill

Figure 19 **Sidestepping**

In sidestepping, weight is transferred from one ski to the other by hip movement. The edges of the skis are set into the hill by rolling the knees uphill to prevent the skis from sliding back down.

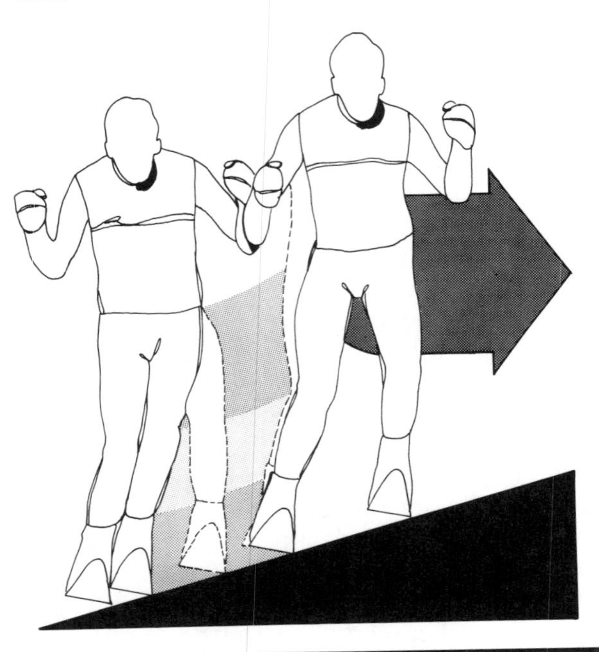

ski has been placed uphill, you must dig the uphill edge of your uphill ski into the hill as you transfer to the uphill ski. This will maintain your position on the hill and prevent sliding back down. Much of the work is done by flexing the knee of your uphill ski as you step up, then straightening that knee to transfer all your weight to the uphill ski. The downhill ski must be lifted, without any weight on it, to come alongside the uphill ski. It is necessary to roll your shoulders uphill as you transfer weight from downhill to uphill ski after you have placed the uphill ski in its new raised position. Note the movement of the shoulder position in **Figure 19** as you transfer weight from downhill to uphill ski. Additional points to note are: use your poles for balance; keep your skis perpendicular to the hill to prevent advancing forward or backward. Just as it is easier to learn sideslipping on a steep slope, it is easier to learn sidestepping on a gentle one.

Stopping

For survival, stopping is the first goal of every skier. Aside from falling, stopping is accomplished by either turning your skis across the hill to lie perpendicular to the slope, or by placing your skis in a snowplow position with your weight on the inside edges of your skis. The basic action for stopping is edging; controlling the edges of your skis so they can bite the snow.

The wedge or snowplow stop is something you probably learned when you first started skiing. It's a stop that skiers of every level must use when moving on a narrow trail or a ski-lift-line and there is no room to turn. For novices, it's the easiest stop to perform because it does not require a turn. The snowplow turn starts by placing your ski tips together and pushing your heels apart. But to make the snowplow work, you must also have your skis positioned on their inside edges. If the skis are too flat, they won't stop quickly enough. The wedge will work with your knees extended or flexed, but to be most effective, flexing the knees and rolling them inward towards each other lets the edges dig deeper into the snow to provide quicker deceleration and stopping. It's OK if your knees are touching **[Figure 20].**

The "hockey stop," performed by turning your body across the hill and skidding your skis to a stop, can be performed with either extended or flexed knees. Novice skiers tend to stop by extending their downhill knee, which works. However, by flexing both knees and angulating them inward (uphill), a greater degree of knee angulation can be obtained and better control of slowing and stopping is realized.

Having focused your attention on flexing your knees to perform a hockey stop, be aware that there is also a place for extending your knees when stopping. Once your knees are flexed, you can increase the pressure on your edges by extending your knees. The increased edge pressure provides you with more force to stop, thereby stop-

Wedge (or snowplow) stop

Figure 20

From a wedge (or snowplow) position while facing down the fall line, movement is begun by separating the knees to flatten the skis on the snow. To slow down and stop, turn the skis onto their inside edges by pushing the knees toward each other as well as pushing the knees forward. Feel your shins press against your boot tops.

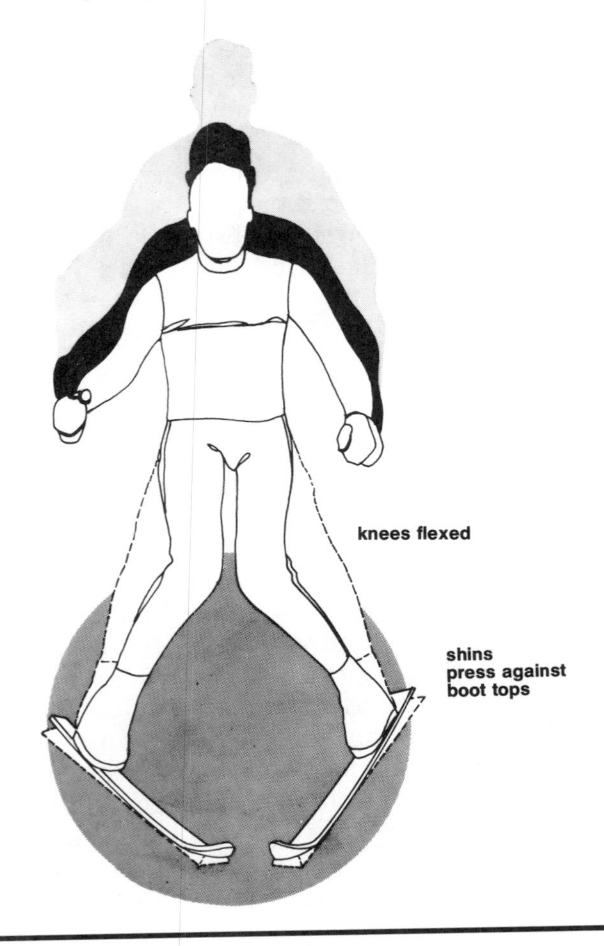

ping faster **[Figure 21]**.

To summarize the actions in a hockey stop, turn your skis across the slope, flex your knees and angulate them into the hill. As you slow down, extend your knees until you stop completely.

Steering to a stop is the slow gentle form of the

Parallel (Hockey) stop

Figure 21

A basic parallel turn is begun with 1) down-UP pressure release; 2) foot twist; and 3) edging the skis until they sideslip to a stop.

Figure 22

Steering to a stop

With the skis facing downhill, both knees are flexed and angulated to one side. In addition, an attempt is made to twist the feet and legs in the direction of the turn. As the skis change direction, a sideslip and check is needed to stop. This is done by increasing knee angulation and edgeset.

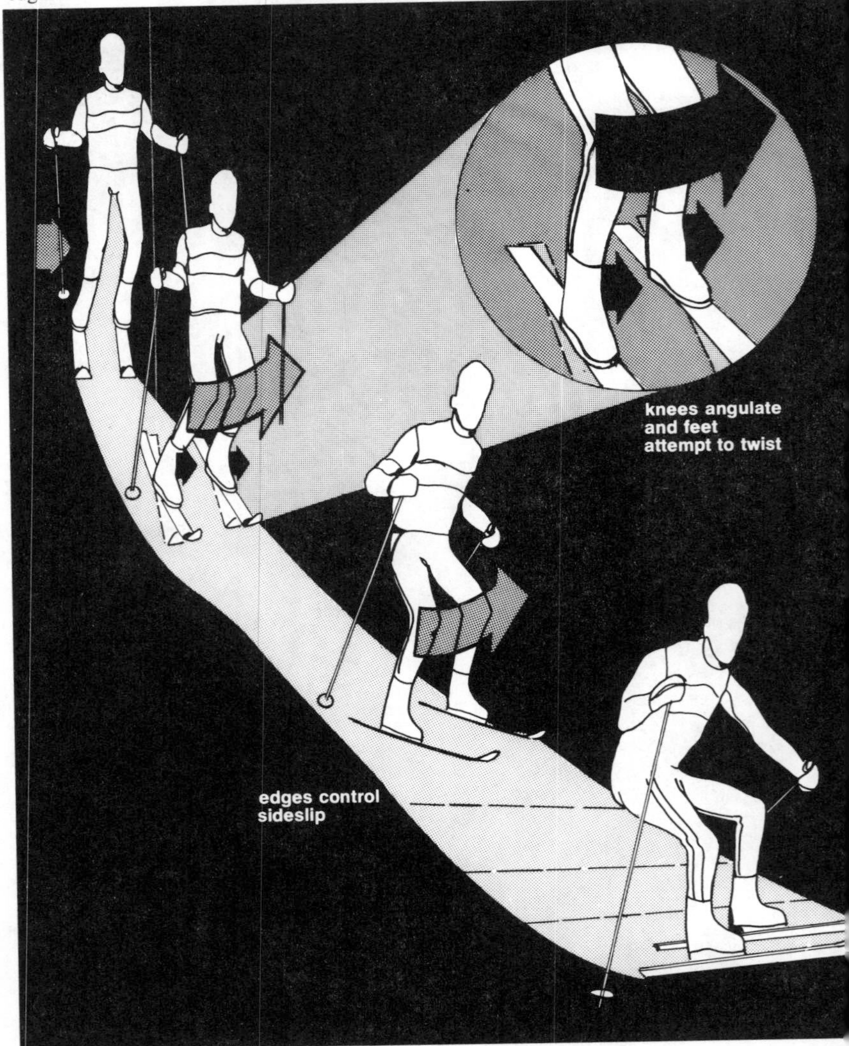

hockey stop. It is performed by transferring weight to a turning ski which has its knee flexed and angulated to its inside edge. Sideslipping proceeds as the ski continues to pivot to lie across the hill. If the turn is proceeding to slowly, a twisting action can be exerted on the turning ski to rotate it faster **[Figure 22]**.

Skidding and Carving

In addition to controlling speed and stopping, edging is used to complete turns. All turns are completed on the ski edges by following either the arc of a curved ski (carving) or the side of the ski (skidding*). The difference between carving and skidding is the degree of edgeset. With the skis barely on edge, skidding with sideways movement results; with an increase in degree of edging, sideways movement is checked and the skis move forward, following the arc in the edged ski, carving. In practice, most turns finish with some element of both carving and skidding (See Figures 7&8, pages 19 and 20).

Knee angulation is the primary action that will stop a skid and convert it to a carve. In many situations, straight knees prevent enough edging to carve, so that the skis simply slide sideways downhill. Flexing the knees permit them to angulate, thereby increasing their degree of edging and permitting them to hold the snow to stop sideslipping or skidding (See Chapter 2: Anatomy of a turn). If you are having trouble carving on steep slopes, check your knees for enough knee angulation.

**Skidding is the combination of sideslipping plus rotation of the tails of the skis around the tips because the tails are slipping faster than the tips. Skidding is achieved with a little more weight forward on the ski tips, and less weight backward on the tails. Sideslipping is a straight downhill sideways movement of the skis with tips and tails slipping at the same speed by equaling weighting tips and tails.*

Figure 23

Wedge turn

From a gliding wedge position with the skis flat, flex your turning knee and push that leg forward against the boot top. Then, roll the turning knee inward and drop your shoulder over the edged ski. As the outside ski begins carving a turn, keep the inside ski flat and minimally weighted.

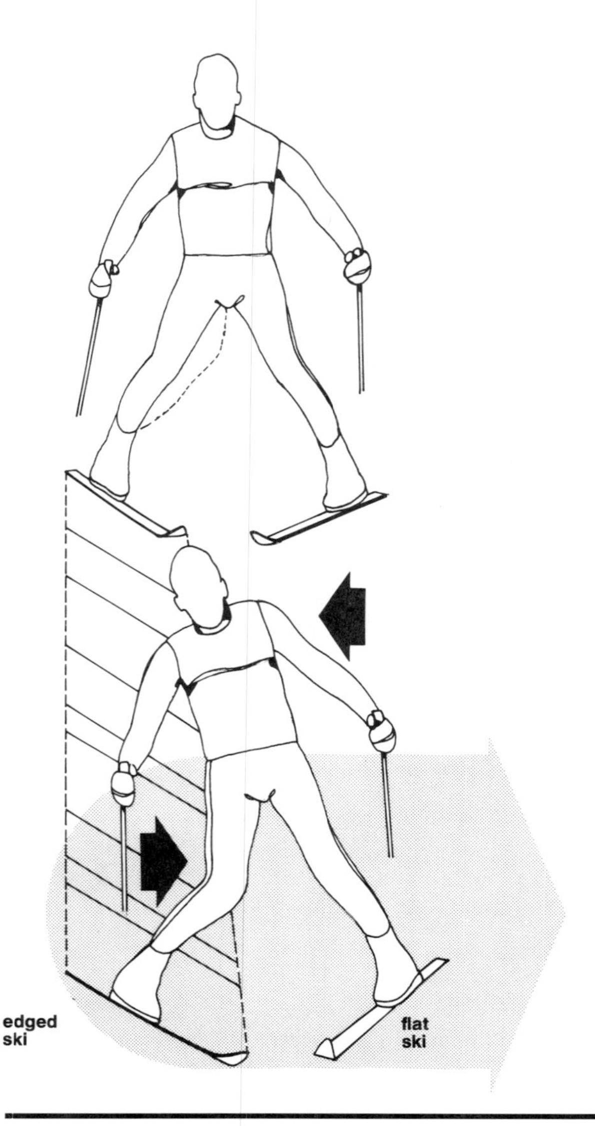

Wedge and stem turns—turning by edging

As noted above, turns are completed on the edges of the skis. The simplest way to turn is to set one ski on its inside edge, pointed in the direction you wish to turn, and then put pressure on that ski by transferring your weight to it. Your turn occurs simply by holding pressure on the inside edge of that ski until your skis cross the fall line facing in the new direction. This is a stem turn; it is a turn on one leg. The stem part of the turn refers only to the beginning half of the turn. The turn is completed by either skidding or carving, depending on how great or small is the degree of edging of the turning ski **[Figure 23]**.

Similarly, if you are in a wedge (or snowplow) position with your tips together and tails apart, by edging your turning ski and putting pressure on it by transferring your weight to it, you will begin a turn **[Figure 23]**.

The two places to improve your stem and wedge turns are:

1. flexing and angulating the knee of your turning ski
2. transferring most of your weight early in the turn to the turning ski.

Knee angulation: Although you can edge with your knee straight, the stem will be more effective and the amount of edgeset greater if your knee is angulated inward. To do this, the knee must first be flexed. Angulating the knee of the turning ski provides a more effective stem turn with better control and a greater degree of edgeset than is achievable with a straight knee.

Weight transfer: A ski on edge is not effective in turning unless there is pressure on the ski; and the greater the pressure, the sharper and more effective the turn. It is important to transfer most of your weight to the stemmed ski at the beginning of the turn, otherwise, the turn will not commence. Some teachers stress transferring all of your weight to the stemmed ski, and even lifting the inside ski off the snow to make sure there is no weight on it. This is an effective method and works well for many skiers and racers. However, it is not necessary to transfer 100% of your weight, and it certainly is not necessary to lift the unweighted ski off the snow routinely. These are teaching points to emphasize that stem turns are one-legged turns and most of your weight belongs on that ski. When stem turning, I often keep a little weight on my inside ski to keep it from drifting off line.

Racers, on the other hand, frequently use stem turns precisely because they are one-legged turns. This gives them the advantage of putting 100% of their weight on the turning ski to get maximum pressure and maximum carving action in the turn with minimum skidding. Racers often perform the stem by stepping from one ski to the other (so called "step turn"), lifting the inside ski well off the snow to insure maximum pressure on their turning ski. The racer's goal is high speed. On the other hand, recreational skiers are usually employing stem turns to slow down. You needn't copy the racers. Keep a little weight on the uphill ski and advance the tip of the uphill ski a little ahead of the turning ski.

Stem turns are also used in situations where sudden pressure changes on the ski edges can be hazardous, such as on ice or breakable crust. In such conditions, pressure on the stemmed ski is applied gradually and carefully to prevent the edge of the weighted ski from breaking through a crusty layer of snow. (This is discussed more completely in Chapter 14: Difficult Conditions).

Uphill and downhill stems

Stemming the uphill ski is a **turning** maneuver. It will turn your skis' direction across the fall line. Stemming the downhill ski is a **braking** maneuver, turning your skis further in the direction they are now facing, further away from the fall line.

Uphill stem: Stem turns begin by keeping all your weight on your downhill ski while pushing the tail of your uphill ski outward; the two ski tips stay together while the tails separate.. The uphill ski is set on its inside edge by rolling its knee inward. When positioned, transfer your weight from the downhill ski to the edged uphill ski. To effectively turn, two points should be observed:

1. The uphill, stemmed ski should be on its inside edge
2. Most of your weight must be transferred to this turning ski.

Downhill stem: The downhill stem is done when traversing a hill and you wish to slow down. Since your weight is already on the downhill ski, to stem this ski push your downhill knee forward, pushing your shin into the top of your boot. This increases the weight on the tip of your ski and reduces the weight on the tail. As a result, the tip holds the snow while the tail is free to skid which reduces speed by turning you uphill.

The downhill stem is controlled by rolling the knee of that ski inward to increase edgeset and convert the skid to a carve; or outward, flattening the ski to let it skid. The action of the downhill leg in the stem is similar to the action of this leg when traversing with parallel skis. Rolling the knees uphill turns the skis uphill.

Practice your stem turns to note edge control, knee angulation, and ability to turn on one ski. However, don't stay in the stem mode too long. The sooner you learn to release pressure and pivot, the sooner you will advance into parallel skiing and controlling steep and bumpy slopes.

Edge control with the wedge

The wedge or snow plow stop is a basic action that you probably learned early (also called "pizza" for youngsters). Putting the tips of your skis together and spreading the tails apart puts your skis in a wedge to stop or turn. If you are an intermediate skier, you probably know how to use the wedge. However, the reason for bringing up the wedge at the intermediate level is the wedge is an excellent position from which to study how your knees control your edges; particularly, how much more control you have with your knees bent (flexed) rather than straight (extended).

Have you ever positioned your skis in a wedge and found you couldn't stop? Why? How does the wedge slow you down? What is the mechanism for turning? The answer is edges. Positioning your skis in the wedge posi-

Garlands *Figure 24*

Garlands get their name from the flower pattern they make in the snow. Garlands are exercises to help learn checking. The actions are traverse, sideslip, and check. Beginning from the traverse with the knees flexed, the knees roll downhill to flatten the skis and begin a sideslip. The sideslip is checked by the knees rolling back uphill to re-edge the skis.

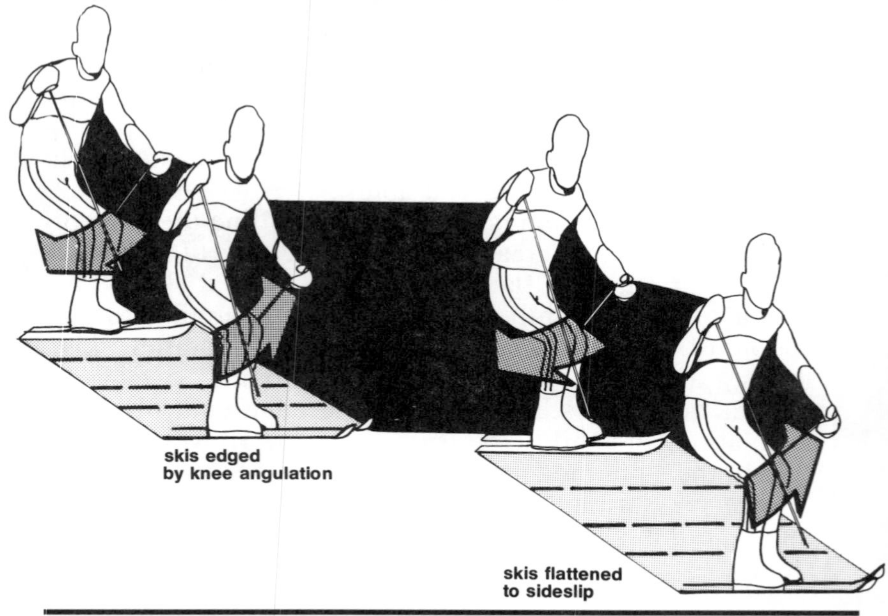

tion does little if the skis remain flat on the snow. To be effective, the skis must be on their inside edges. It is the edges of the skis biting the snow that turns you and slows you down.

Beginning, intermediate, and expert skiers all use the wedge at certain times. However, observation of each type of skier discloses differences. Beginners usually hold their knees stiff, have their skis flat on the snow, and experience very slow responses to their efforts to turn or stop. Advanced skiers will use one of two positions: either the knees are straight, the tails of the skis wide apart, and the skis on their inside edges; or their knees are flexed and angulated inward, the tails not so wide apart, and the skis are on their inside edges. Either way, the common denominator is the skis on their inside edges.

The secret of a good wedge is knowing how to flatten and edge the skis. Lying on their bottoms the skis slide and accelerate; resting on inside edges the skis turn or brake. Edges are set either by widely separating the tails of the skis with straight knees or narrowly spreading the tails (about 24 inches) and flexing and angulating the knees inward. To accelerate with straight knees, the tails must be pulled closer together to flatten the skis, which requires quite a bit of effort. In contrast, if the knees are already flexed and angulated, it is quite easy to flatten the skis by simply deangulating the knees while keeping them flexed.

After experimenting with the two ways to wedge, straight knees or flexed knees, concentrate on the flexed knee method. With your knees bent and tails a comfortable distance apart, try to control your ski edges by rolling your knees together to slow down and rolling them apart to speed up. When your skis are edged to slow down, note that by increasing the pressure on your skis by extending your knees a little, you can regulate the degree of deceleration. This is an important lesson. If you can feel your knees control your edges in a wedge position, you will be able to easily transfer this feeling to parallel skis **[Figure 20]**.

Turning with a wedge is simply a matter of weight shift and increasing pressure. Transferring weight or increasing pressure by extending the knee slightly to one of the edged skis makes that the turning ski. You will turn in the direction that ski is pointing.

Your upper body follows the direction of your skis. You don't need your ski poles when using the wedge. If you have poles, hold them at your sides so they don't get in the way. To make the turn sharper, angulate the knee of the turning ski inward to help carve the completion of the turn.

Garlands

A good exercise to learn edge control is performing garlands. The term comes from the pattern the skis leave in the snow which look like the flower of the same name **[Figure 24]**. In a traverse across a moderately steep slope, alternately roll your edges into the hill, then release them; roll your knees, then release. Each time you release the edges you sideslip; as you increase the degree of knee angulation uphill, the sideslip is checked.

Chapter 6

Balance

Fore/Aft balance
Weight forward versus backwards
Hands and Poles
Balance between the two feet
Weighting the downhill (or turning) ski
Minor points:
  Advancing your uphill ski
  Touching the knees together

Summary: Proper body stance has two requirements:

1. **Flexed knees**
2. **Appropriate weight distribution fore and aft on your skis**

Knee flexion, the first requirement for knee angulation and edge control, lowers your seat and puts your weight back on your heels. It must be balanced by ankle flexion, pushing your shins against your boot tops, to keep your weight centered. Because knees can flex more than ankles, further increased knee flexion must be balanced by bending forward at the waist.

After edge control, balance is the next basic skill to acquire in skiing. Balance is proper body stance, which in skiing is dynamic, always changing. It includes how you distribute your weight on your ski and how you distribute your weight between your two feet. This is important for the beginner, intermediate, and expert. As you ski faster, link your turns closer together, and ski on more challenging terrain, fore-aft and side-to-side balance becomes more critical.

Fore/Aft balance

Good balance is vital to good skiing. Fore/aft balance is controlled by knee flexion, ankle flexion, and waist flexion **[Figure 25]**. Balance begins with the prerequisite

Figure 25 **Fore/aft balance**

The three factors that affect weight distribution between heels and balls of feet are knee flexion, ankle flexion, and waist flexion.

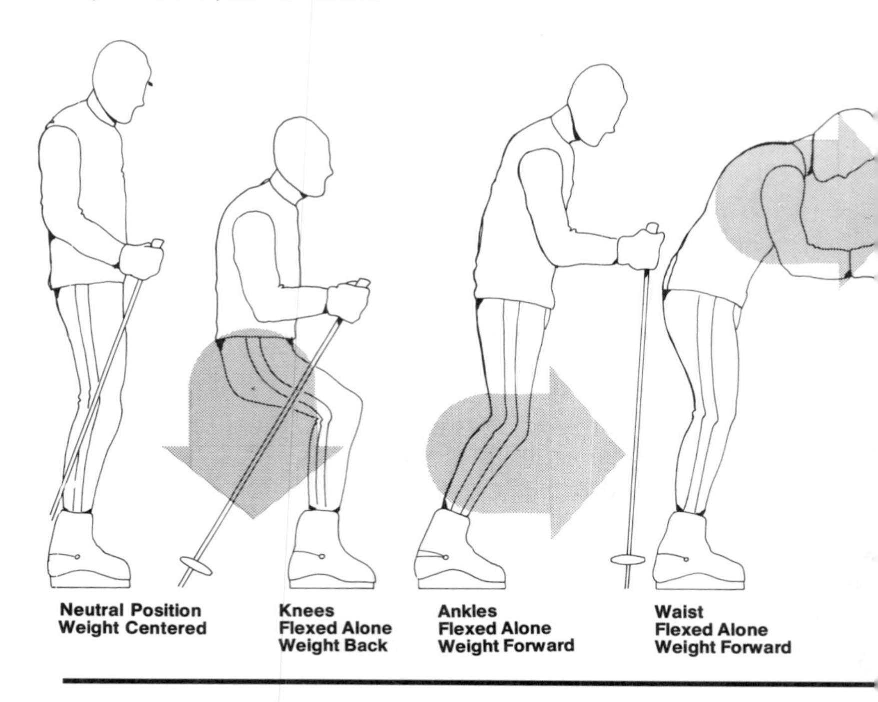

that your knees should be flexed to permit edge control by knee angulation. Knee flexion alone drops your seat and puts your weight on your heels. To prevent sitting back, skiers flex their knees by **pushing the knees forward**, feeling the shins pushing against the boot tops, which automatically flexes the ankles. Combining knee flexion with ankle flexion results in centering your weight over the skis to maintain your balance **[Figure 26]**. Finally, the knees can flex much further than the ankles, so that increased knee flexion will again throw your weight back on your seat. This is balanced by bending forward at the waist. Thus, when the knees are flexed, balance is maintained first by ankle flexion and then by waist flexion. Waist flexion is used only when the ankles are fully flexed and more forward balance is needed. A simple rule of

Balancing knee flexion *Figure 26*

Coordinating flexion of the knee, ankle, and waist maintains a balanced position with the weight centered on the feet. **A)** Knee and ankle flexion are balanced permitting the weight to be centered. **B)** Increased knee flexion transfers the weight back to the heels. **C)** From the unstable position in B, the only way to get more weight forward is to bend at the waist.

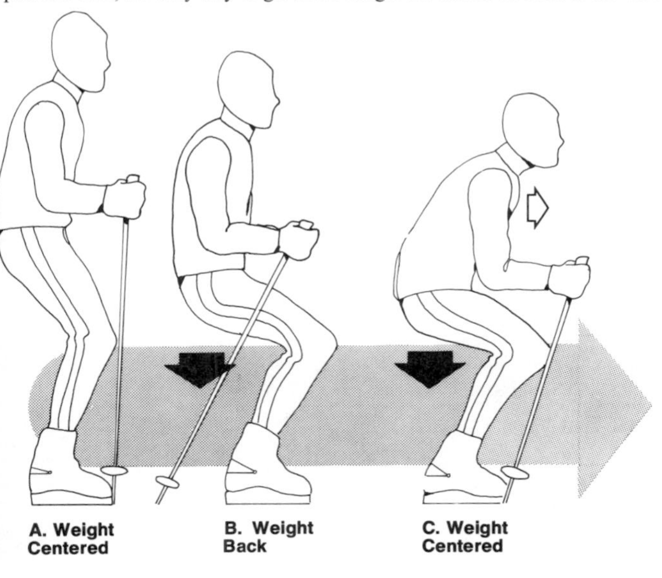

thumb to get started is to flex your knees by dropping your seat over your heels. This will automatically combine ankle and knee flexion to maintain fairly good balance **[Figure 27]**.

Weight forward versus backwards

While skiing, your weight is constantly changing from the middle of your feet to a little forward and a little backward. These dynamic (moving) changes are normal. To make a sharper turn, one with a smaller radius, put more weight on the balls of your feet and less weight on the heels by tilting your body forward at the beginning of the turn. Also push your knees forward to feel more pressure of your shins against your boot tops. As you complete the turn, shift your weight back to center by easing the

Figure 27 **Balance–seat over heels**

All the positions shown here are proper stances. They each fulfill the criteria of having some knee flexion and maintaining equal weight distribution between heels and balls of the feet. In **A** and **B**, each degree of knee flexion is balanced by a corresponding degree of ankle flexion. In **C**, with 90 degrees of knee flexion, waist flexion must be added to ankle flexion to maintain proper balance because ankle flexion cannot transfer as much weight forward as knee flexion transfers backward.

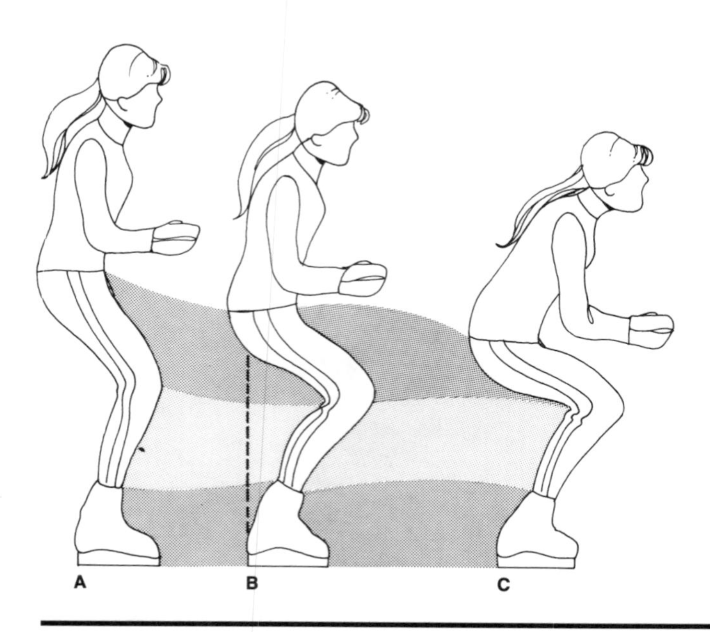

pressure on your boot tops. The reason for putting weight forward is to increase pressure on the ski tips. This frees the tails of the skis to pivot around the tips (skidding) to complete the turn in a shorter distance. Once the turn is complete, easing your weight back to center spreads the pressure evenly across the skis edges and stops the pivoting. The skis can then follow their tips forward and proceed into the next turn.

How much weight to exert forward is determined by trial and error. In general, the steeper the slope the more forward pressure you want to feel. When linking a series a fast turns, you want to keep your weight forward all the time, always feeling your weight pushing against your boot tops. You will also feel weight on the balls of your feet and toes but little weight on your heels. In contrast, on gentle slopes when performing long radius turns, there is no need to push your weight hard against your boot tops. Your weight can remain centered, tips and tails of skis evenly pressured, as there is not a need for the tails to pivot around tips; the skis can gradually turn by carving with minimal skidding. (See Chapter 2: Anatomy of a turn.)

Hands and Poles

Hands and poles are other minor but important contributors to balance. When skiing, both hands should remain in front of you so they are always in your vision. The hands and poles are additional items that help keep your weight forward.

Balance between the two feet

It is certainly easier to balance on two feet than on one. There are times when more weight will fall on one ski or the other. In general, when traversing, more weight falls on the downhill ski; when skiing straight downhill, weight is equally distributed; when turning, most weight will transfer to the turning ski (or outside ski, which will become the inside ski at the completion of the turn). When turning rapidly from side to side, weight will constantly shift from one outside ski to the other.

Weighting the downhill (or turning) ski

On packed slopes, turning is more efficient and more effective if you transfer most of your weight to the downhill or turning ski. Lifting your inside ski is stressed by some instructors as a technic to make sure you have 100% of your weight on the downhill ski. For racers this is important; it puts all of your weight on the turning ski to give it maximum carving ability and reduce skidding. The fraction of a second saved can mean the difference between first place and tenth place in some races. However, in recreational skiing seldom is "maximum" carving performance essential. More often your goal in a turn is to reduce speed rather than accelerate. Once you have learned to transfer your weight to the turning ski, keep the uphill ski on the snow with a little weight remaining on it to keep it in its track and prevent it from wandering and crossing.

In deep powder, powder at least 20 inches deep, the physics of skiing changes and deep powder skiing requires equally weighted skis. As will be explained further in the chapter on powder, the depth to which skis sink into deep powder is directly related to the amount of weight on them. Placing more of your weight on the downhill ski results in the two skis sinking to different levels in the snow which makes skiing more difficult. This phenomenon does not occur on packed slopes where you can place all your weight on the downhill ski and the skis remain on the same level.

Minor points:

Advancing your uphill ski a couple of inches ahead of the downhill ski is a maneuver that helps keep your shoulders downhill. The more you traverse perpendicular to the fall line the more important this is; the closer you are to skiing straight down the fall line the less important.

Touching the knees together is a habit I have found helpful. While some instructors advise against this because it inhibits independent leg action, I seldom find it a problem. The advantage of locking the knees together is that it permits one leg to feel what the other is doing. Particularly when turning to a rapid rhythm, keeping the knees touching helps the skis turn simultaneously and reduces the tips crossing. Try skiing with your knees touching and with them a little apart. Use what feels most comfortable to you.

Do not flex knees too early after the up motion. Following your pole plant and down-UP pressure release, do not begin the down motion for the completion of that turn until your skis have crossed the fall line. This will help you use that down action for the beginning of your next turn.

CHAPTER 7

Pressure Control

Pressure release by down-UP movement
Down motion for pressure release
Leg retraction
Pressure release over a mogul

Summary: Pressure control is a group of actions designed to lighten your skis to facilitate turning or to increase weight on your skis to permit edge control. This is most important on steep, bumpy, and powder slopes. It is not as important on gentle slopes. There are 4 ways to release pressure:

1. **Down-UP–this is a down motion, flexing your knees, followed by a quick UP motion. The up motion should be performed without straightening the knees.**
2. **Down–a quick drop of your seat over your heals.**
3. **Leg retraction–the most difficult method of pressure release is performed by tightening abdominal muscles and lifting the knees upward.**
4. **Skiing over a bump, mogul, or rough terrain releases pressure. Increasing pressure to increase edge control is performed by extending your knees.**

On steep and bumpy slopes, short radius, quick turns are needed to control speed and balance. While initiating quick turns is possible by simply transferring weight from one ski to the other, this sometimes does not achieve a full, 180° turn quickly enough. To accomplish a faster, short radius, 180° turn, pivoting both feet together is often the only technique that works well. And, to pivot both feet together, there must be a moment in which simultaneously there is very little weight or pressure on both feet. This moment of weightlessness is realized by releasing the pressure from your feet (unweighting is the old term).

If you do not pivot both feet together, there is little need to release pressure form your skis. On gentle slopes, where wide arc turns are very effective, pressure release is not required because pivoting both feet together is unnecessary. Effective turns are accomplished simply by shifting weight and balance from one foot to the other, increasing pressure on the turning ski by extending it, rolling the ski edges from side to side, or stem turning.

Releasing pressure can be achieved in several ways: Hopping up; quickly sinking down by flexing your knees; tightening your abdominal muscles and lifting your knees up (called leg retraction); or simply skiing over a bump and finding your ski tips and tails airborne and weightless. Although there are a variety of ways to release pressure, the simplest and easiest to learn is hopping up.

Pressure release by down-UP movement

Hopping to release pressure is performed by bending your knees and quickly hopping up, lifting your seat one or two inches. You cannot lift your seat to lighten your feet if your knees are straight; flexed knees are a necessary preliminary action. The preliminary flexing of the knees drops your seat down a few inches, and to emphasize the importance of dropping the seat down before it is suddenly lifted up, this type of pressure release is often referred to as down-UP release. The "up" is emphasized because it is the up action that actually does the pressure releasing; the down action is just preparation. While the down motion can be slow or fast, the up action must be quick to permit significant pressure release **[Figure 28]**.

The preparatory down movement has two roles: first, it provides a platform from which the “UP” motion can rise; second, it permits the UP motion to occur without straightening the knees completely. The UP motion is quick, but short in distance. Because you should always be skiing with a little flexion in your knees, the down motion begins with your knees already flexed. From this position, you drop your seat down a couple of inches and then quickly lift it UP the same couple of inches, but no more. This will keep your knees partially flexed to facilitate edging your skis to complete your turn.

Down-Up pressure release *Figure 28*

From an upright position with the knees slightly flexed, knee flexion is increased by dropping your seat down, over your heels (down motion). Plant the pole after the down motion. This signals the UP motion which should be quick.

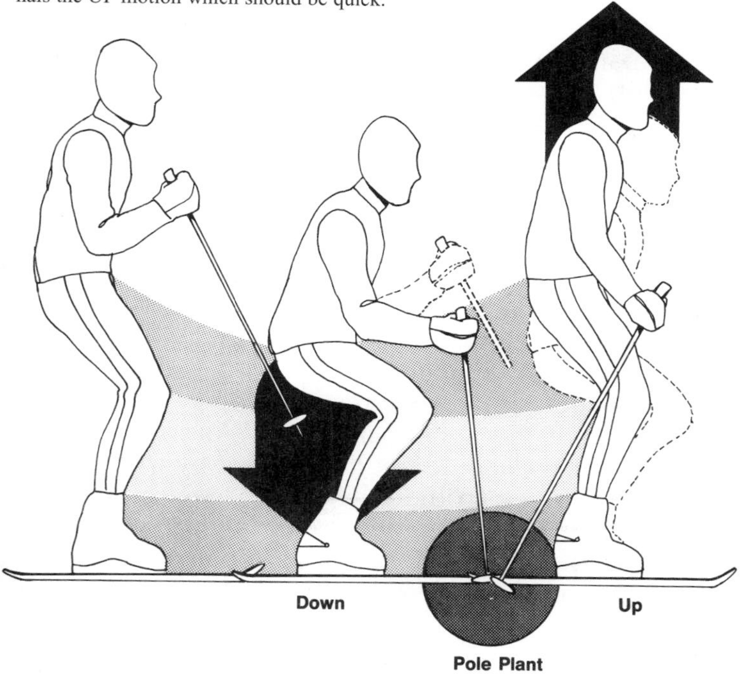

One of the common errors in down-UP pressure release is completely straightening (extending) the knees on the UP motion. This makes it more difficult to reset the edges quickly.

The down-UP concept is well known to most skiers. However, some are unaware that the purpose of the down-UP action is simply to allow both skis to pivot easily at the initiation of a turn. If following your down-UP action you transfer your weight from one foot to the other rather than pivoting your two feet simultaneously, you require little if any down-UP movement.

Failure to release pressure from both feet simultaneously often stems from fear of losing contact with the ground, even for a split second. One way to allay this fear is by proper use of the ski pole. The primary purpose of the ski pole is to stabilize your body at the moment of pressure release from your skis. By planting your pole in the snow just before you lift up, you anchor your hand, arm, and upper body to the ground. This is your security blanket; this is your contact with the snow when your weight is off your feet. When you are skiing by simply transferring weight from foot to foot without feeling a moment of weightlessness, there is very little need for the pole plant other than to emphasize timing.

Timing the pole plant is important. The sequence of actions is 1. Down; 2. Pole plant; 3. UP. With practice, these three actions can be performed rapidly, within one second. But although they may appear to be performed simultaneously, the appearance is deceiving. They are being performed in sequence.

Deep powder skiing requires that you keep your feet equally weighted throughout each turn. As a result, turns in deep powder are should not be initiated by transferring weight from one leg to the other; they require either an edge change of both skis simultaneously, or a pivot of both feet together. To perform these, a down-UP motion to release pressure on the skis is required at the initiation of each turn.

Perhaps the commonest reason for intermediate skiers remaining at the intermediate level is the inability to learn pressure release. Even if you go through the motions of dropping your seat down and lifting it up before you turn, if as you rise up you simply step from one ski to the other you have totally missed the point.

Transferring weight from one ski to the other (the old stem-christie) is not releasing pressure from both feet; it will not permit a free pivot of both feet simultaneously and quickly. While the transferring of weight from one leg to the other works well on gentle slopes or when long radius turns are desired, it is not effective in deep powder and may be less effective on difficult terrain, particularly when you wish to make quick, sharp angled pivots, to enable you to cross the fall line without gaining speed.

Exercise to feel pressure release

There are some exercises that can help you learn to release pressure. One of the easiest is to plant both poles in the snow a little in front of you. Leaning on both poles, flex both knees and quickly lift your seat hard enough to lift both heels off the ground. The tails of the skis will lift off the ground too. The feeling you experience at the moment your heels are off the ground is the feeling of weightlessness. Remember it. This is the same feeling you want to experience when releasing pressure to turn.

Other ways to release pressure: Down-UP is the first and most important technic of releasing pressure. Other methods are a quick drop of your seat down, going over a bump, and leg retraction.

Down motion for pressure release

The simple act of squatting, flexing your knees by dropping your seat, will momentarily release the pressure on your skis and reduce the weight on your feet. The down action is very much like the quick bend of your knee that occurs when you walk barefoot on a beach and step on a sharp stone. Your knee flexes quickly to take pressure and weight off your foot. The down motion for pressure release is the same type of sudden drop, using both knees. The down motion to release pressure can be described as a quick lowering of your seat **[Figure 29]**. Once the turn has begun, slowly return your seat to its previous position by extending your legs from their acutely flexed position to raise your seat.

Each time you flex your knees while skiing you experience some pressure release of your skis. In fact, when you drop your seat as you complete a turn, you are partially releasing pressure from your feet which makes it easier to finish the turn.

The primary advantage of the down motion for pressure release is at the "moment of truth"– that is, the moment of maximum pressure release from your skis–your body position is ideal for turning and edge control because:

Figure 29 **Down pressure release**

From an upright position, the pole is planted and you drop your seat down suddenly. To be effective, the down motion must be fast.

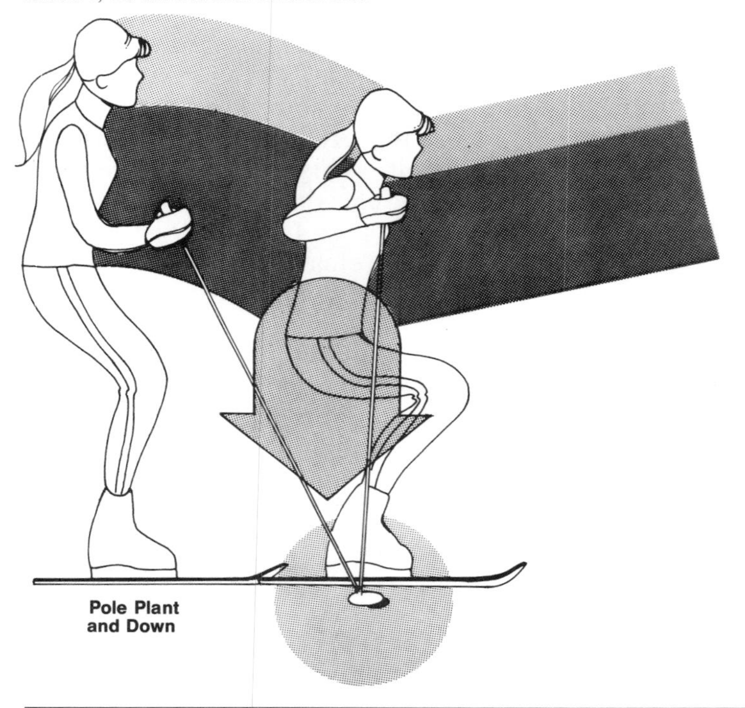

1. Knee flexion is at its greatest, thereby permitting maximum knee angulation for edging
2. The center of gravity is lowest, providing maximum stability, particularly with increased knee angulation.
3. Completion of the turn is easier since the completion movement of the turn is slow extension of the legs.

Practice the down motion at home

You can demonstrate the down action for pressure release at home by standing on a bathroom scale and watching the weight indicator. Standing upright on the scale, quickly drop your seat over your heels by bending your knees forward. The weight on the scale will decrease. The quicker you squat, the faster is the weight reduction. A slow descent will reduce weight minimally over a prolonged time while a rapid drop will reduce weight to a greater extent, but over a shorter period of time.

Leg retraction

Leg retraction is the quickest, most efficient, and smoothest way to release pressure. This is also the most difficult way. It is performed from a knee flexed position by quickly tensing your abdominal muscles and simultaneously lifting your knees upwards. Another way to think of this is by lifting your heels beneath your seat. The action that lifts the heels is also lifting your knees straight up–towards your chin **[Figure 30]**.

Leg retraction lifts the weight of the legs from the ground without lifting the feet off the ground. Leg retraction is often preceded by a down-motion so it can be described as having a down-UP rhythm. However, in the usual down-UP pressure release, the upper body is pushed up by the legs; in leg retraction the legs are lifted upwards by the upper body. In the usual down-UP motion, the legs do all the work; in leg retraction the abdominal, thigh, and back muscles also must work. It takes much less energy for the leg and thigh muscles to push up than for the upper body muscles to lift up. Thus leg retraction is the most demanding and tiring form of quick pressure release.

The advantage of leg retraction is it permits you to release pressure expeditiously with almost imperceptible vertical motion. Preparation by the upper body is by isometric contraction of abdominal muscles which is quicker than either down or up actions. Pressure release occurs by increasing knee flexion with a quick action that is followed, almost immediately, by automatic extension of the legs when the muscle tension is released. By leg retracting on top of a mogul, the automatic extension occurs on the down side of the mogul, just when you want it to occur to help you increase pressure and edge your skis as you complete the turn. The quickness of this whole action lets you complete turns rapidly so you can turn again on the same mogul if you wish.

Figure 30 **Leg retraction**

First a preparatory down motion flexes your knees and lowers your seat. Then, pressure release is performed by simultaneously tightening your abdominal muscles and pulling your knees upward. Your upper body leans slightly forward at the waist.

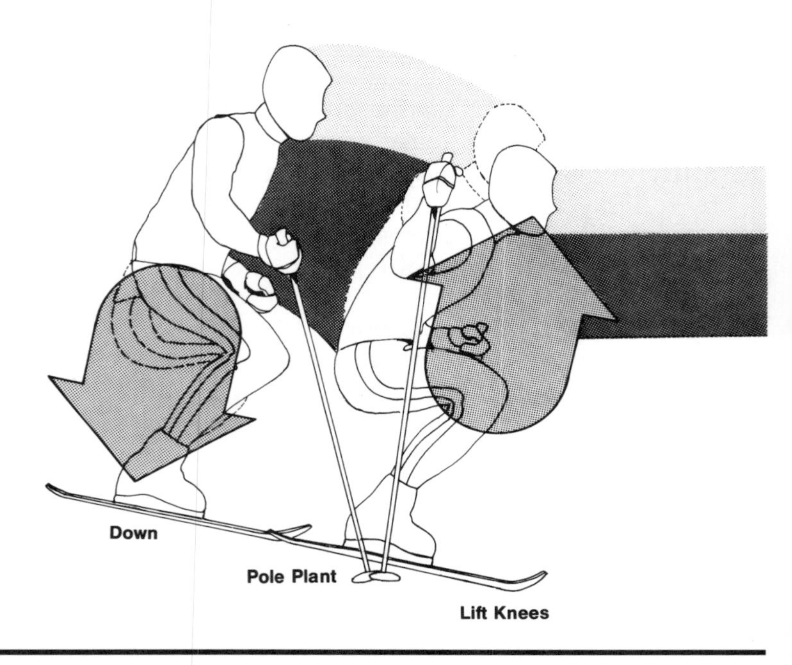

Differentiate between down-release and leg retraction

It is important to recognize the difference between the simple down motion alone for pressure release and leg retraction. When down releasing the moment of pressure release occurs while the seat is dropping down. In contrast, when leg retracting, most of the pressure release occurs after the seat is down. The muscle action is also different. In down releasing, the seat is lowered by relaxing the thigh muscles, so the work is performed by gravity. With leg retraction, the body must do more work to lift the legs against the pull of gravity. Leg retraction is performed by contracting the abdominal and hip flexor muscles. The abdominal muscles, with aid of a pole plant, steady the upper body while the hip flexors lift the legs *

Anatomy of leg retraction *Figure 31*

A) The muscles that retract the legs are the thigh flexors. The iliacus and psoas muscles attach to the femur together, in a single tendon. The rectus femoris is a weaker muscle. **B)** With the leg and thigh straight, the thigh flexors must do more work. **C)** With the hip flexed 90°, the muscles that flex the thigh have a better mechanical advantage. However, the iliopsoas is still pivoting a bone 14 to 18 inches long by pulling only 4 or 5 inches from the hinge. This is why leg retraction requires more strength and energy than other types of pressure release.

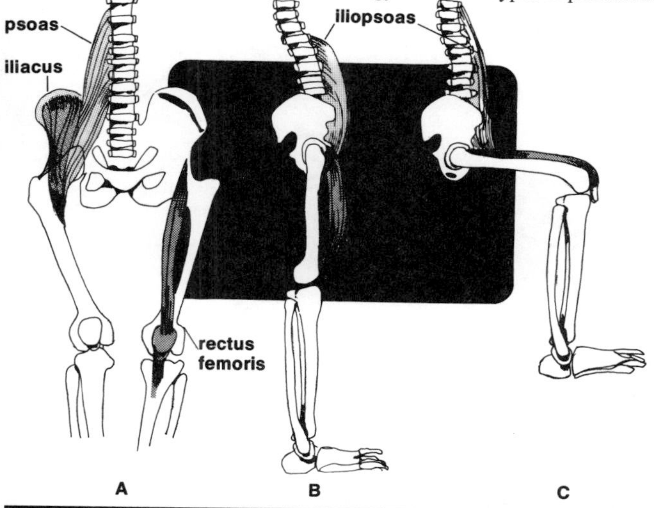

Leg retraction can be performed from any degree of flexion, but it is more efficient when the knees and thighs are deeply flexed, close to 90 degrees. In this position, the hip flexors have a better mechanical advantage from which to lift the knees **[Figure 31]**.

Because lifting your knees up tends to throw your weight back, leg retracting is accompanied by a short, quick flex of the waist forward to keep your weight balanced. There are two reasons for the body weight being forced backwards with leg retraction: First, lifting the legs up from a flexed position rotates the body backwards around an axis running through the hips **[Figure 32]**. Second, the muscles that extend the legs (the quadriceps) are stretched when the knees are flexed. Lifting the knees stretches them even further.

**The strongest hip flexors are the iliopsoas muscles. These muscles run from the lower spine bones (lumbar vertebrae) to the thigh bones (femurs). The rectus femoris muscle is another hip flexor (Figure 31).*

Figure 32 **Leg retraction rotates weight backwards**

Leg retraction rotates the body's weight backward on an axis through the hips. To counteract this force, the upper body leans forward at the waist.

Thus, when pressure from the feet is released, the stretched leg extensors shorten. In doing so, they advance the lower legs and feet, producing a "jetting" motion of the feet forward **[Figure 33]** which in turn throws your weight back on your heels.

Leg retraction from a knee-extended position, that is with your knees straight, requires that you first drop your seat a few inches in preparation for leg retracting. If you flex your knees quickly and then leg retract, you will experience a combination of pressure release by both down-releasing and leg retracting. If you slowly flex your knees you will not get much release from the down action. If you stay constantly in a knee-flexed position you get no release from the down motion but you will be able to turn faster and have a quicker sequence of your turns.

Practice leg retraction in doors between chairs

Leg retraction can be felt indoors by supporting your weight with extended arms on the backs of two chairs. In order to lift both feet simultaneously off the ground, you must tighten your belly muscles and lift your knees up. Notice that it is easier to perform if your knees are bent.

Stretched extensor muscles *Figure 33*

Leg retraction puts additional stretch on the extensor muscles of the legs (quadriceps). Releasing pressure from the feet releases the stretched muscles which causes the feet to jet forward.

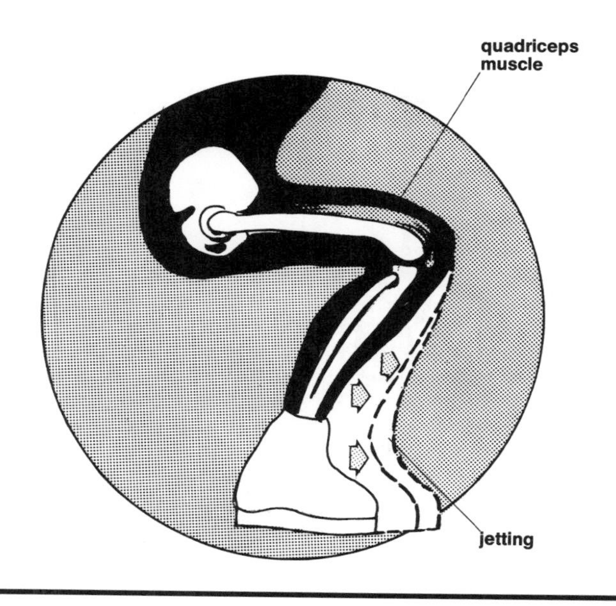

As a matter of fact, if you hold your knees perfectly straight you can't raise your feet off the ground. Flexed knees are a necessary prerequisite to leg retraction **[Figure 34]**.

Pressure release over a mogul

The easiest way to release pressure is by simply skiing over the crest of a mogul. At the moment your feet pass the peak of the mogul, your ski tips and tails are suspended in air and have no weight on them **[Figure 35]**. At this instant you can pivot your feet or simply shift weight from your downhill to your uphill ski. Either way, pivoting or transferring weight from foot to foot, you will produce an easy turn, although a longer radius turn. This is a passive way to turn without releasing pressure under your feet by either actively lifting or dropping your weight down. The terrain actually does the work for you.

Figure 34 **Leg retracting with 2 chairs**

You can feel leg retraction by suspending yourself between two chairs and holding your arms straight. Lifting your knees up is similar to leg retraction.

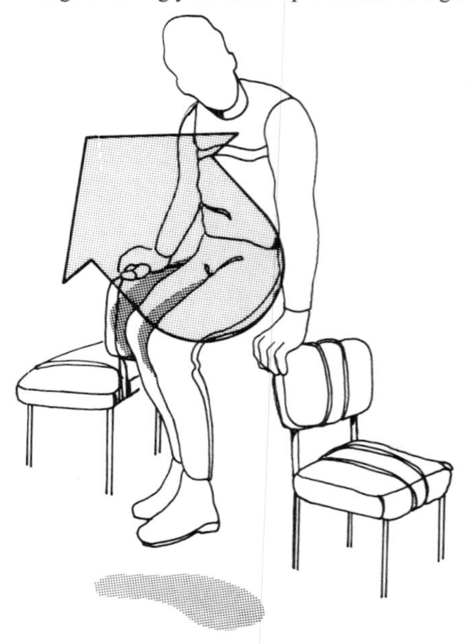

However, this type of turning does not allow quick, short radius, 180° turns. It will work on small moguls and moguls on gentle slopes but it may not be as effective on steep moguls. On steep moguls you may need a bigger pivot, the kind you can only produce with active pressure release.

Pressure release on a mogul

Figure 35

On a mogul, the tips and tails of the skis are suspended in air and are free to pivot. Just beyond the crest, the downside of the mogul will move away from the skis, thereby releasing pressure from them.

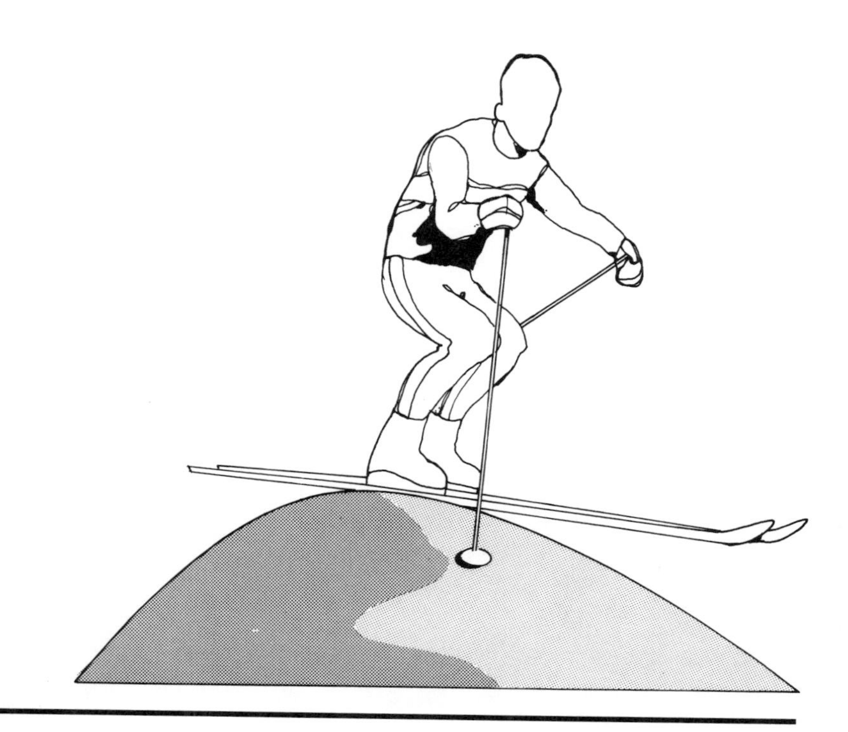

Chapter 8

Rotation

Foot rotation
Shoulder Rotation with the Turn
Shoulder Rotation Before the Turn--Anticipation
No Shoulder Rotation (continuous anticipation)
Exercises to maintain shoulders facing downhill
Hip rotation
Knee rotation
Steering

Summary: Rotation of feet and shoulders are primary turning forces. Foot rotation is a twisting of the feet during pressure release. Shoulder rotation during a turn helps change direction to get the skis to face across the slope. Advanced skiers have their shoulders rotated to face downhill before turning, a move called anticipation. The most efficient way of turning quickly and efficiently is to keep the shoulders and upper body facing downhill all the time; the lower body pivots to one side, then the other, with each turn.

As mentioned earlier, two turning forces can change the direction of the skis: Edging the skis to follow the arc of the skis; and rotation, a circular movement around the long axis of the body. Picture a person standing straight, with a long flagpole running from the head to a point between the two feet **[Figure 36]**. Throwing one shoulder forward and the other backward will turn the body around the flagpole in a circle. This circular movement about a central axis is rotation.

Four parts of the body may rotate when skiing: The feet, knees, hips, and shoulders. The most important of these are the feet and shoulders.

Figure 36 **Rotating on Body's Long Axis**

Rotation is pivoting the body around its long axis, which runs from the center of the head to between the feet. Rotation can be performed by arms, hips, knees, or feet.

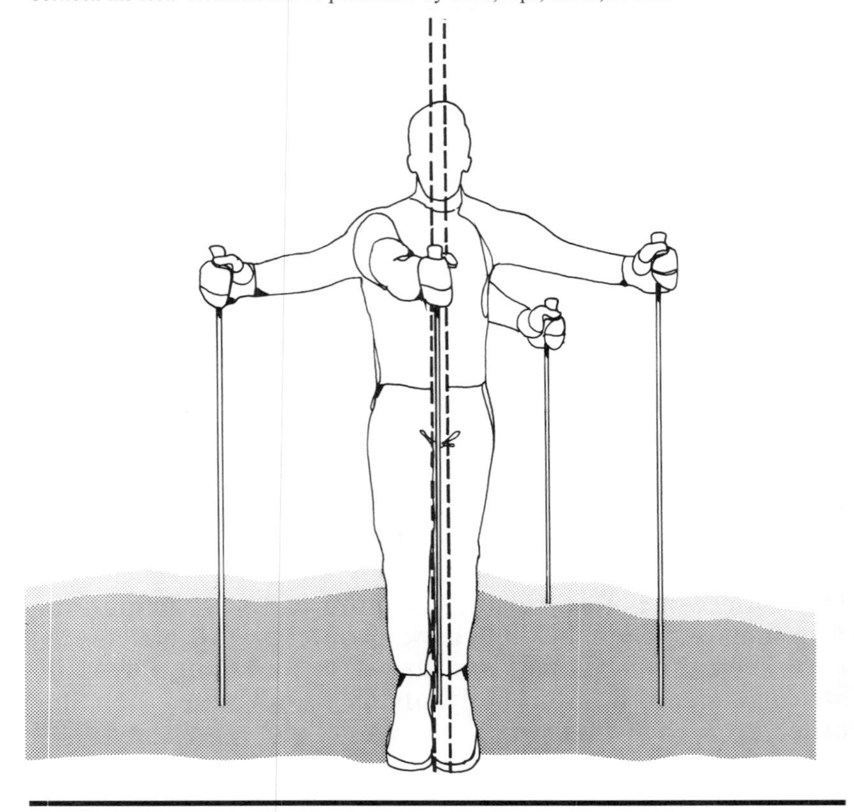

Foot Rotation

Foot rotation is often called foot twist, swivel, or pivot. The feet rotate by action of the leg muscles below the knees. However, when standing on skis, foot rotation is difficult because of the body's weight putting pressure on the skis. Foot twist is possible only if there is pressure release at the moment of the twist. Riding on a chair lift is an excellent way to feel the action of foot twist. Here there is no weight on your feet and the skis have no pressure at all on them.

Foot twist without pressure on skis *Figure 37*

Foot rotation can be felt and observed while riding a chair lift. With your hands resting above your knees, twist your feet from side to side without moving your knees or thighs. This is the same muscle action that is used in foot twist.

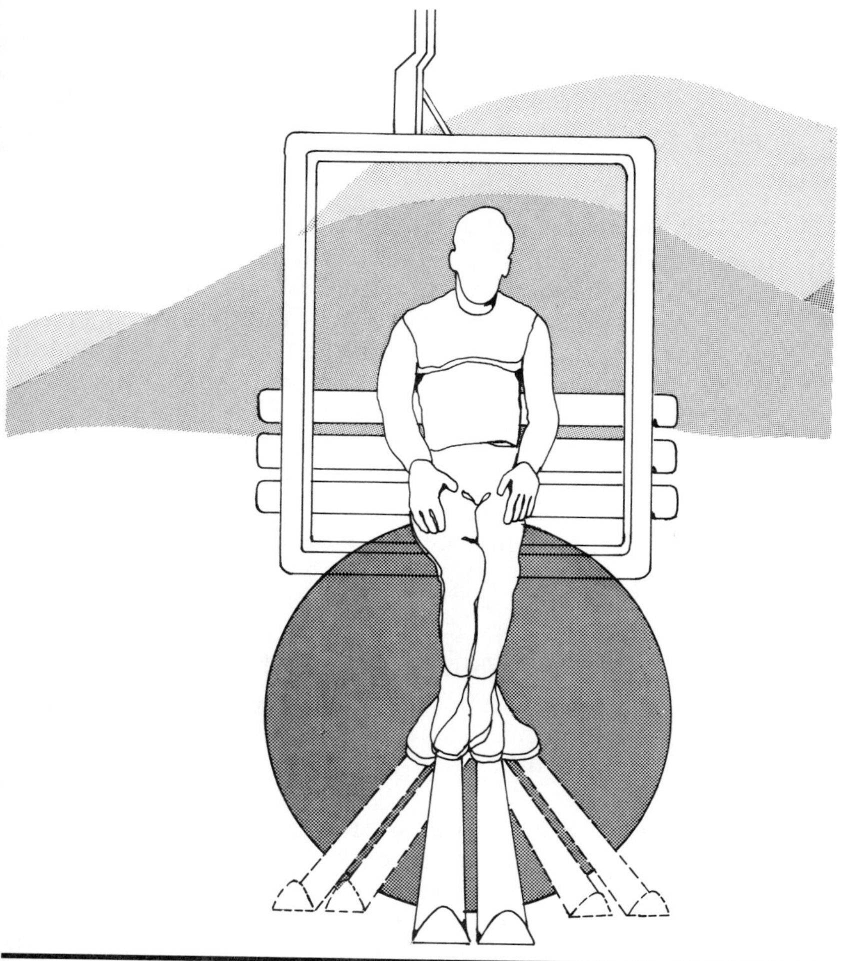

The feet can now be twisted in either direction without moving the hips or knees **[Figure 37]**. On the lift you can observe that foot rotation is limited to about 15^0 . When more turning is required, foot twist is combined with other forms of rotation.

Shoulder rotation: the shoulders can rotate with the turn, before the turn, or do not have to rotate at all.

Shoulder Rotation with the Turn

Rotating your shoulders and arms in the direction of a turn is a major turning force. After skiing a few times you have probably learned that rotating your arms and shoulders is a reliable way to turn your skis across the hill to reduce your speed. As the skis begin to change direction, rotation of the arms and shoulders in that direction greatly accelerates the turn.

The mechanism by which rotating your arms and shoulders turn your skis is the long muscles of your trunk, particularly the muscles that run in your abdomen and along your spine. You can feel this force indoors, standing up, with your feet firmly on the floor. As you stand erect, knees straight, and arms at your side, raise your arms straight away from your sides to a 90° angle from your body **[Figure 36]**. Next, rotate your arms and shoulders in either direction and note how your belly muscles feel stretched and tight. If you now quickly rotate your arms forcefully to one side you will feel your feet rotating against the floor to point in the same direction as your shoulders.

The same thing happens on skis. If you rotate your arms and shoulders through a turn, the long muscles of your trunk will twist your lower body and your skis in the same direction. Thus, rotating your shoulders with a turn is a common technic used at beginner and intermediate levels.

However, while shoulder rotation with a turn will work for single turns, it prevents linking together a series of quick turns. It is fine for wide arc turns, but is too slow for fast, short radius turns, the type you need on steep or bumpy slopes. On difficult terrain, completing turns with shoulder rotation takes too much time.

Shoulder Rotation Before the Turn--Anticipation

Rotating your shoulders to face downhill before the skis begin turning is called anticipation because the upper body is looking ahead anticipating the direction of the next turn. Anticipation can be performed long before the next turn begins. By rotating your shoulders downhill, you stretch the muscles that connect your thighs to your upper body (abdominal and back muscles). This is similar to stretching a rubber band between two points. When your legs release pressure from the snow, your muscles shorten automatically, twisting your feet to face downhill. Your feet are now pointing in the same direction as your upper body which remained fixed. This action is similar to the shortening of the stretched rubber band when one end is released (See Figure 11, page 27).

To feel anticipation, traverse a slope and, prior to turning, rotate your shoulders so they face down the fall line. You should feel your belly muscles stretching and tightening as your feet face in one direction and your shoulders and hips face in another. (If you don't feel your belly muscles tighten you are not rotating your shoulders far enough). From this twisted position you initiate your turn by planting your pole and momentarily releasing pressure from your skis by a down-UP motion. The instant you release the pressure on your skis from their grip on the snow, your stretched body muscles will shorten, rotating your legs and skis to face in the same direction as your shoulders. This is an automatic body response that requires no active energy on your part. You supplied the energy before the turn when you rotated your shoulders downhill.

The rotation of the skis to the fall line is quick, and momentum has been generated to carry the skis past the fall line to face in the opposite direction. You can accentuate the degree of turning in this direction by pivoting your feet.

Until this moment, your turn was performed entirely by your lower body rotating beneath your non-rotating upper body. If you haven't slowed down enough, you can reduce your speed in one of two ways: Edge your skis firmly into the hill with knee and/or hip angulation; or rotate your shoulders in the new direction. If you rotate your shoulders through the turn, you will then have to rotate them again, in the opposite direction, to face them downhill in preparation for the next turn. However, if you can control your speed by knee angulation alone, your shoulders can remain facing downhill and you will immediately be prepared to turn again.

No shoulder rotation (continuous anticipation)

Maintaining your shoulders facing down the fall line all the time gives you the power of shoulder rotation without actively rotating your shoulders. Each time your legs pivot to the side while your shoulders remain facing downhill, the long body muscles are twisted and tightened. You have the same torque, or rotating force, that you create by rotating your shoulders downhill while the legs remain facing across the hill. However, if you can achieve this turning force by pivoting just your legs while your shoulders remain still, you will utilize less energy and be able to turn more quickly. In effect, you will develop the advanced technic of skiing straight down the fall line with only your lower body and skis rotating from side to side. Your upper body will remain relatively still.

It is possible to keep your shoulders constantly facing downhill only if you are able to control your speed with your knees (and sometimes your hips). If you can't, you will need your shoulders to rotate through the turn to slow down; then you will not be ready to start the next turn.

There is a common explanation for intermediate skiers who can wedel with their shoulders fixed downhill on gentle, flat slopes, but can't do it on steep slopes or moguls. On gentle slopes, the turn itself is enough of a slowing mechanism that no additional speed reduction is required. Therefore it is not necessary to angulate your knees into the hill or to rotate your shoulders through the turn to further reduce speed. You can simply hold your shoulders facing downhill while you release pressure and pivot from one side to the other.

Moguls and steep slopes require more work to slow down than gentle slopes. Quick pivoting of your skis is not enough. You must also edge your skis or rotate your shoulders uphill to reduce your speed. If you can’t do it with your knees, you must do it with shoulder rotation--for survival! The result is your shoulders are facing across the hill unprepared for the next turn. Your rhythm of continuous turns has been interrupted.

Once you discover that you can control your turns with your knees alone, you may need help in breaking the habit of rotating your shoulders through each turn, even though it is no longer necessary. Here are a couple of reminders to help keep your shoulders facing downhill:

1. As you complete a turn, concentrate on keeping your turning shoulder (outside shoulder) back.
2. As you plant your pole to turn, release the pole by pushing your wrist forward and keeping that hand and shoulder leading your turn. As your skis go through a turn, first reaching the fall line, then turning away from it, you should feel your belly muscles relax momentarily half way through the turn, then tighten again as the lower body continues to rotate while the shouders remain facing downhill.
3. Caution: When keeping your turning shoulder (outside shoulder) back so it does not rotate through the turn; do not hold your hand and pole down, behind you. Keep both hands in front of you, elbows bent. It is only the shoulder that needs to be held back. (See Chapter 9: Poles and Arms).

Overturning should be avoided. Overturning is rotating your shoulders through a turn so hard that your skis turn too far uphill. This causes too much slowing down and stops your turning momentum. The next turn becomes more difficult to perform. Overturning can be avoided by not rotating your shoulders with each turn.

Better skiing requires that you maintain your shoulders continuously facing downhill while your lower body rotates from one side to the other. The upper body and lower body look in different directions at the beginning and completion of each turn. Only at one short moment, during the middle of each turn, are the shoulders and skis pointing in the same direction; that moment is when the skis are pointing straight downhill. The rest of the time, the shoulders are fixed facing downhill while the skis are continuously changing their direction, from one side of the fall line to the other. Even though the shoulders are not actively rotating, the rotational forces of the long body muscles are working in the same way as when the shoulders do rotate with each turn.

One way to view your body is to compare it to a child's outdoor swing. The chains supporting the swing are fixed while the seat is free. If you twist the seat 90^0 around the chains and then release the seat, it will untwist to return to its neutral position. The momentum of untwisting will rotate the seat beyond neutral, in the opposite direction. When it stops rotating in the opposite direction, it will untwist again towards neutral.

In skiing, your upper body can be compared to the chains of the swing and your lower body compared to the seat. If your upper body faces downhill while your lower body (and skis) face across the hill, the long muscles of your body are twisted and stretched. The moment you lighten the weight on your feet (down-UP), you release your skis to pivot (like releasing the seat of the swing). The long, twisted muscles of your body will straighten and shorten, acting like a spring, rotating your skis downhill to face in the same direction as your upper body. The momentum of the skis' rotation will carry them across the fall line to start to pivot uphill in the opposite direction. By actively twisting just your feet in this new direction, you can complete the turn of the skis to the other side without rotating your shoulders. And just as important, as your skis turn back uphill, by keeping your upper body fixed facing downhill, the long muscles of your body twist again, so they automatically are ready to repeat uncoiling the moment you release pressure from your feet for the next turn.

Exercises to maintain shoulders facing downhill

There are some exercises to help you learn to keep your upper body facing down the fall line while your feet face across the hill:

1. Traverse a gentle hill. Rotate and hold your shoulders and upper body facing down the fall line all the time. Feel your downhill shoulder pulled back, and at

the same time, keep your poles infront of your body. Every few seconds, angulate your knees into the hill and feel your abdominal muscles tighten as your skis turn further uphill, while your upper body remains facing down the fall line. As you feel yourself slow down, de-angulate your knees to stop turning uphill, and traverse further. You will feel partial relaxation of your abdominal muscles. Repeat this sequence several times; knee angulation into the hill slows you down while reducing knee angulation lets you speed up. Concentrate on the tight feeling of your abdominal muscles as you twist your shoulders to face down hill while your skis move at a right angle to your upper body. This exercise is also good practice for knee angulating. After traversing the width of the slope, turn in the opposite direction and practice the same thing the other way.

2. On a gentle, flat slope, ski straight down the fall line with your poles held in both hands in front of you. Establish a wedeln rhythm of:

a) Down-UP pressure release with quick, short lifts of your seat and
b) Pivot both feet in one direction
c) Simultaneously move your poles in the opposite direction, still holding your poles straight in front of your body and your body fixed facing down the fall line.
d) Continuously repeat these actions to a regular rhythm. In performing this exercise, you feel like you are doing "The Twist" on a dance floor with both feet twisting in one direction and your hips, arms, and shoulders twisting in the opposite direction.

There is asynchronism between upper and lower body.

In skiing, the principle of fixing the shoulders facing downhill is most important when initiating turns on steep and bumpy slopes. When turns are initiated by rolling edges, shifting weight, or stemming, quick pivoting is not necessary. On gentle slopes when long radius turns are used, it makes little difference whether the shoulders face downhill all the time or remain facing in the direction of the skis.

Figure 38 **Hip projection**

Hip projection is rotating your hips while simultaneously lifting your outside hip. This de-angulates your hips, flattens your skis, and makes it easier for the skis to rotate. It also gives your hips more turning power because they can swing in a wider arc.

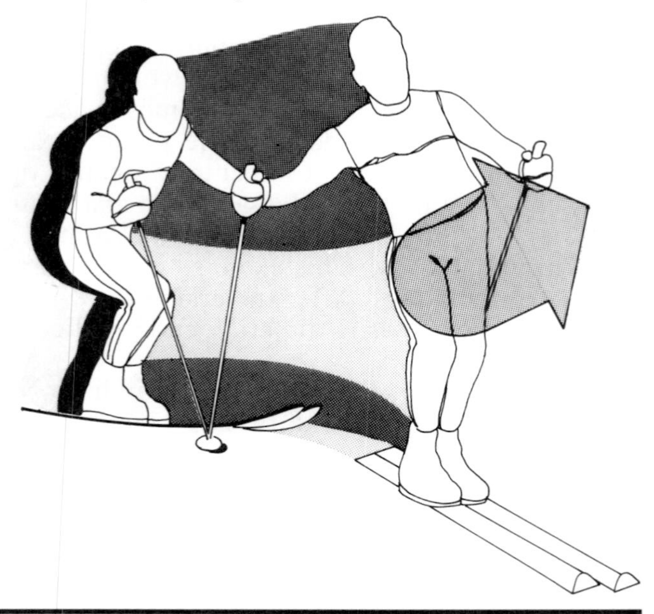

Hip rotation

Hip rotation is used as an additional turning force to supplement foot rotation and anticipation when stronger rotational forces are needed. Although a small degree of hip rotation passively accompanies anticipation, hip rotation should not be regarded as a basic element of anticipation.

Hip rotation is reserved for difficult snow conditions such as deep, heavy powder and crust. It can be accentuated by lifting your hip up when releasing pressure by a down-UP motion, to bring your skis closer to the surface of the snow. Lifting the outside hip tilts the pelvis, moving the hips laterally, away from the center of the turn (it is the reverse of hip angulation). This hip movement is called hip projection, because the hip is thrown to the outside, giving a wider arc in which to generate more turning power **[Figure 38]**. Hip projection flattens the skis against the slope, eliminating edging. This permits the skis to pivot more easily, but it also prevents edge control. Therefore, it is important that hip projection be used only to initiate a turn and then be reversed once the turn has started, by leaning the hips inward, towards the center of the turn. This is essential to permit knee and hip angulation to edge the skis and complete the turn.

Steering *Figure 39*

Steering is a combination of foot and lower leg rotation with knee angulation. This is an extremely important method of executing small changes in direction without releasing pressure. It combines the basic elements of skidding and carving

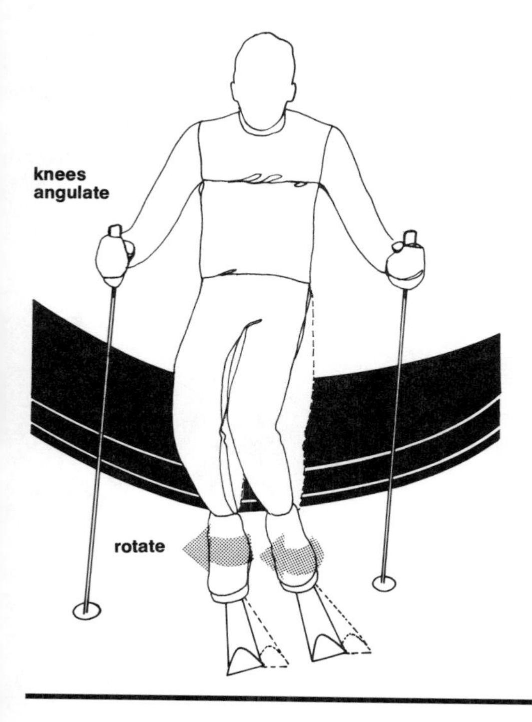

Knee rotation

Knee rotation in skiing is a minor action of little significance. The knees act primarily as a hinge joint with forward and backward movement only. When the knees are extended (straight), they cannot rotate or twist. When flexed, the knees are capable of a little rotation which supplements foot rotation and knee angulation.

Steering*

Steering is guiding the direction of the skis by a combination of knee angulation (edging) and lower leg rotation. It produces gentle changes in direction without releasing pressure or shifting weight.

Steering is performed with the knees flexed. The knees are pushed inwards, in the direction of the turn, to edge the skis. Simultaneously, the leg muscles try to twist the feet in the same direction **[Figure 39]**. Because there is pressure on the feet, they will not turn or pivot quickly; instead they will turn gradually.

Thus, these forces will gently turn the skis by a combination of carving and skidding. Steering is usually performed by the two legs simultaneously, but can also be executed by one leg alone. Steering can assist in completing a turn, provide a long radius turn itself, or be used to initiate a stop (See Figure 22, page 50).

** Steering was first described by G. Joubert and J. Vuarnet, "How to ski the new French way" New York, Dial Press 1967.*

Chapter 9

Poles and arms

Summary: The arms and poles should be held in front of your body. Their purpose is to help maintain balance during the moment of pressure release. Therefore, the pole should be planted just before pressure is released. The pole should be planted with the wrist and released by bending the wrist forward as your body advances beyond the point of the pole plant.

Ski poles are a timing device and, more important, a mechanism to stabilize your body during that unstable moment of pressure release. Since the main purpose of the poles is to act as a stabilizer during pressure release, you really don't need your poles until you start releasing pressure. When stem turning, wedge turning, or rolling your edges to turn, you do not need a pole plant. Children, particularly, do better without their poles until they reach the point of parallel turns.

While skiing, your arms should be held comfortably in front of your body with the elbows bent The poles should be planted in the snow primarily with wrist action and only a little shoulder action. Once the pole is planted, you will quickly ski past that point in the snow where the pole tip is fixed.

The pole should be released by flexing your wrist downward so the pole can easily lift out of the snow as you ski past it **[Figure 40]**. If you maintain the pole plant in the snow after your body has passed the pole tip, your shoulders will inadvertently be rotated through the turn so they face uphill, a position you want to avoid. Once the shoulders are pointing uphill, you are out of position to immediately proceed into the next turn.

To avoid releasing the pole too late, plant the pole by flexing the wrist upward; then consciously flex your wrist downward, pushing the pole in front of you, as you ski past the pole. Your arm and shoulder should remain in place; only your wrist should bend as you move past the planted pole

Figure 40 **Pole plant using wrists**

Your wrist is cocked up to plant your pole ahead of your foot. The pole is released by skiing past the basket and bending your wrist downward and forward. Your shoulder should not fall behind the line of your back.

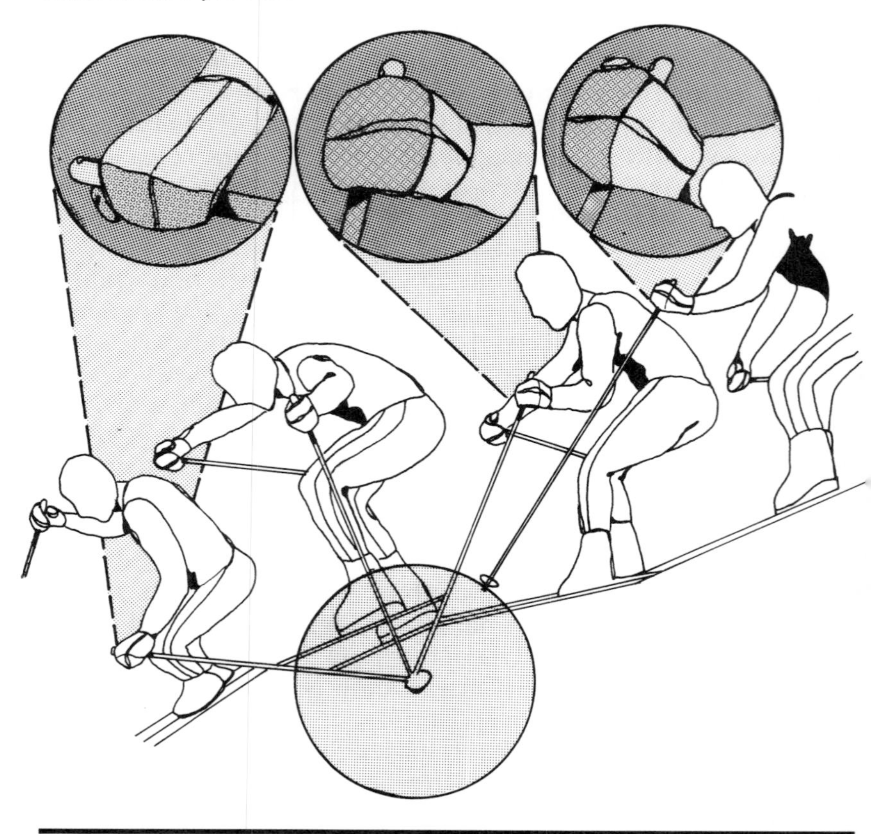

basket. By keeping your arm in front of your body and flexing your wrist downward, the pole will release quickly without holding back your inside shoulder. In turn, this will prevent the pole plant from accidently rotating your shoulders through the turn.

The point in the snow where you plant the pole is not as important as the way you plant the pole. Don't reach forward with your arm or shoulder; this will rotate your shoulders toward your ski tips, untwisting your body muscles which were ready to help you pivot. Instead, lift your wrist up and plant the pole with a flick of your wrist in the direction of the fall line. If you are traversing so that your skis are almost perpendicular to the fall line, plant the pole a comfortable distance in front of your foot. If your shoulders are facing downhill, plant the pole at the level of your foot. After it is planted, push the hand and arm of the planted pole straight downhill with your wrist; keep the hand and arm leading the way through the turn so your shoulders do not rotate uphill at the end of the turn.

On gentle slopes, you do not need your poles as much as you do on steep slopes and in moguls. On difficult terrain, the position and use of the arms and poles becomes quite important. In general, your arms should be held in front of your body and to the side. Your hands should be held at the level of your shoulders so the poles can hang straight down without accidently touching the snow; your elbows should be flexed. When making a continuous sequence of turns down the fall line of difficult terrain, it is helpful to maintain both poles in front of your body all the time. The turning pole is planted with just your wrist, aiming for a comfortable spot to the side. The spot is chosen because you can reach it with your wrist alone, with minimal movement of your arm and shoulder and keeping the arm in front of your body, pointing downhill. After planting the pole, the arm remains in front of your body; the wrist flexes and lifts the pole out before the pole can pull your arm back. The pole remains in front of your body while you make your next turn with the other pole. By keeping both poles in front, you are ready to quickly plant and release the pole in rapid succession to help time your turns in rapid succession.

Keeping the poles in front of your body has an extra benefit; it helps you keep your forward-backward balance, especially in mogul fields. This is one more aide in keeping your weight forward, to avoid being thrust backward as you ascend a mogul.

Double pole plants

In difficult, heavy snow, simultaneously planting both poles can assist you lifting both heels out of the snow to start a turn. The two poles are planted, one on each side of your skis; a vigorous down-UP motion lifts your skis out of the snow where they pivot; and the poles are simultaneously released by bending your wrists forward.

Part II

Putting it all together

Chapter 10
Gentle smooth slopes

Where to learn
Order of learning
Short skis
Edge control
Traverse with knee angulation
Steering
Parallel turns
Rolling edges--crossovers
The easy turn--pure carved turn--banking
Parallel turns with rotation
Pivoting both feet
Pressure release--Unweighting
Basic parallel turn
Wedeln–get some rhythm
Better parallel turns
Preturn–end of one turn is start of another
Anticipation
Banking
Combining skills
Minor points:
- *Weighting the uphill ski*
- *Lifting your inside ski*
- *Advancing the uphill ski*
- *Knees touching*
- *Leaning foward*

Summary: Smooth gentle slopes are the place to learn to ski as well as learn new technics. The main skills needed on gentle slopes are edging and balance. On gentle slopes you don't have to worry about survival and can focus on improving your skills. Rotation and pressure release skills are not necessary on gentle smooth slopes, but this is the place to develop and perfect these skills.

Where to learn and practice

The best place to learn skiing technics is on a smooth, gentle slope. Here you accelerate gradually, gain speed slowly, and can ski a considerable distance before feeling you are going too fast. This provides the opportunity to concentrate on your technic without worrying about survival.

There is a school of thought that advocates practicing on steep slopes as the best way to learn to handle steep slopes. However, this is not a philosophy I support. Strong and aggressive skiers may eventually master steep slopes by skiing only on them, but this is the hard way to do it. Why kill yourself? Skiing should be fun; enjoy it. The four basic skills of skiing (edging, balancing, pressure control, and rotation) can all be learned and perfected in the safe atmosphere of a gentle slope. Once developed, they can then be applied to more challenging terrain. While learning, it is helpful to ski a run or two each day on a tough slope to feel how much more difficult it is to master steep and bumpy conditions. However, on these slopes intermediate skiers are usually too concerned with survival to concentrate on mastering technic. When the going gets tough, the tendency of most skiers is to use the novice technic of rotating their shoulders uphill to reduce speed instead of flexing and rolling their knees hard into the hill.

On gentle slopes, all techniques are effective: short or long radius turns, one or two legged turns, stem or parallel turns. A good skier knows how to perform each of these because different technics are needed as snow and slope conditions change. You don't need all of them on gentle slopes, but you will want them on moguls and steep slopes. Therefore, to make sure you will have these skills when you need them, practice them on gentle slopes where it's easier to learn.

Order of learning

The first step toward being an advanced skier is being sure you can perform correctly the basic skills of skiing. After that, you can work on variations, timing, and coordination.

Below is a rough progression of skiing skills that can assess where you are on the skiing ladder. These actions need not be learned in precisely this sequence, but this is a reasonable order in which to acquire them. Usually, a few of these are practiced simultaneously because they must be used together, such as pressure release, pole plants, and pivoting. Although used in combinations, it is easier to concentrate on just one action at a time. Spend just a few minutes on one, then go on to another. After working on two or three specific skills, repeat the sequence.

1. Wedge turns and wedge stops
2. Stem turns and hockey stop
3. Edge control with knees for slowing, stopping
4. Steering
5. Sideslipping, carving and skidding
6. Down-UP pressure release to unweight
7. Pole plants
8. Parallel pivoting both skis
9. Anticipation
10. Checking
11. Preturn
12. Banking

Short skis

The "Graduated Length Method" (GLM) was introduced by Cliff Taylor. Its principle is: "The longer the ski, the more difficult it is to turn; conversely, the shorter the ski, the easier it is to turn". This observation is quite applicable to the novice skier. By using short skis when first learning to ski, you can feel the basic actions in skiing quicker than you can with longer, more cumbersome skis. The primary advantage of length in a ski is increased stability when going fast. Since beginners ski slowly, they don't need much length for stability. By using short skis, the beginning skier can more easily master the fundamentals and progress more rapidly up the intermediate ladder. After skiing a few times and gaining enough confidence to ski faster, the length of the ski is increased; hence the name graduated length method.

Edge control

To ski comfortably on any slope you must know to stop. Since the edges of the skis are the essential tool in turning and stopping, learning good edge control is vital for good skiing. Edges can be controlled from either a wedge or parallel position. Learn both ways because there will be times you need each position. (See Chapter 5: Edging: How to use it, for a discussion of edging in the wedge position.)

Traverse with knee angulation for slowing and stopping

Traversing a slope is a good way to bring your skis together and feel the sensation of parallel skiing. By crossing the hill perpendicular to the fall line you will not gain much speed and you can move good distances if the slope is wide. This is a good place to practice edge control with parallel skis. First flex your knees. The best way to do this is to drop your seat directly over your heels. Next, slowly roll your knees uphill. This sets your skis on their edges, turns you slightly uphill, and slows down your speed. If you slow down too much, regain your momentum by rolling your knees in the opposite direction, downhill. This will reverse your uphill turn and begin to turn you downhill. By repeating and repeating this action across the hill many times, you will develop the feeling of edge control for speed control.

In the same traverse, experiment with quickly rolling your knees uphill. This should give you a quick stop. You can now test the effect of knee angulation on speed by trying slow and fast knee rolls into the hill and noting how gradually or how quickly your edges slow you down. (See Figure 18, sideslipping, page 44)

Early intermediate skiers should practice slowing and stopping with both the wedge and parallel skis using knee angulation. The sooner you learn to angulate both knees into the hill with your flexed knees, the sooner you will have mastered the technic for slowing down and survival.

Steering

Steering is a movement that most people discover by themselves. It is simultaneously twisting your feet and angulating your knees in the direction you wish to go. You add steering to your stem turns and parallel turns without thinking much about it. (See Figure 39, page 89)

Steering is an important skill to develop. It is often used when completing turns. A little extra knee angulation or foot twist just before starting the next turn is a form of steering. You are trying to pivot the skis a little more. When skiing in difficult snow conditions such as ice, crust, or powder and you wish to maintain your weight on both skis without shifting much weight, forceful, prolonged steering is often used to slowly change direction with minimal change in pressure on the skis.

Steering is used in powder and packed snow. In addition to rolling your knees in the direction of the turn, steering can also involve pushing your knees forward, pressing your shins against your boot tops. This increases pressure on your ski tips, lightening your tails, so your skis gently pivot around their tips continuing your turn.

Parallel turns

Parallel turns are turns performed with both skis moving together and in unison throughout the turn. Parallel turns are initiated in only one of two ways: either both skis pivot together or their edges roll from one side to the other together. Rolling the edges of the skis with knee angulation, hip angulation, or banking results in long radius, gradual turns. It is used primarily on smooth, gentle slopes. If you never ski on any other type of slopes than smooth and gentle ones, you probably don't need to learn to release pressure and pivot; edge rolling can suffice. However, if you wish to handle steep and difficult terrain proficiently, parallel turns by reducing pressure on your feet (unweighting) and pivoting your skis is required.

Rolling edges–crossovers

Rolling edges is a good method for initiating parallel turns, particularly gentle, gradual turns. Rolling edges is simply changing the edges of both skis from one side to the other. This redirects the curve in the skis in a new direction. In any turn, the skis begin by resting on one set of edges, then rolling from an edged position to lying flat on their bottoms, and finally rolling up on the other set of edges (See Figure 4, edge change, page 15). Since the edges are controlled by your body position, it is your body crossing from one side of the skis to the other that switches the edges. These edge changes have been called crossovers because the body does exactly that.

Crossovers can be performed by the knees, hips, or upper body. This is achieved by rolling your knees from side to side (knee crossovers); shifting your hips from one side to the other (hip crossovers); or banking your body from one side to the other (body crossovers).

The easy turn–pure carved turn–banking–inward lean–"commit"

Gentle slopes provide the opportunity to use the pure carved turn. What does this mean?--A turn that follows the curve in your ski. This turn begins by positioning your skis on their edges and staying on the edges throughout the turn (See Figure 10, carving, page 22). This is a long radius turn with a big arc. You cannot use this turn on steep slopes because you gain too much speed for comfort. Nor can you use this turn in moguls because the peaks and valleys will bounce you all over the slope. However, on gentle slopes the wide-arc carved turn can be the smoothest, easiest, and most energy efficient turn if you use your body correctly.

The pure carved turn is performed by edging your skis with any of the three methods of edging, knee angulation, hip angulation, or banking, or any combination of them. The easiest way to carve is by banking, but you need a little speed to do this. In practice, most carving will be done with a combination of banking plus some knee and hip angulation.

The primary action in starting the pure carved turn is setting the edges of the skis on their sides, pointing in the direction of the turn. The simplest way to do this is by banking your upper body, leaning it inward, in the same way a bicyclist leans inward to turn (See Figure 16, banking, page 40). Another term to describe inward lean is move your center of mass into the turn (or "Commit" for center of mass into the turn*).

Committing yourself to a turn means letting your upper body lean inward and downhill. Once you start to lean, you are committed to staying with this position until the turn is almost completed. I say "almost completed" because after your skis cross the fall line and begin uphill again, you must stop leaning uphill or you will fall. The inward lean is against centrifugal force which diminishes at the completion of a turn. At this point you are ready to straighten up and immediately "Commit" yourself to the next turn and lean in the opposite direction.

Two other elements are important in this turn besides banking:

1. transferring your weight to increase pressure on the turning (outside) ski.
2. initiating the turn with a little down-UP (flexion-extension) action of the knees.

While just leaning inward alone can start a banked turn, such a turn will feel awkward and difficult to control. You must increase the pressure on the inside edge of your outside ski. You do this by increasing pressure on the edges of both skis, but until you become proficient, it is best to focus on putting more weight and pressure on the outside ski alone.

How do you transfer weight to the outside foot? You can't lean toward the outside because you must lean in the opposite direction, inside, to bank the turn. The answer is to straighten or extend the outside knee while keeping the inside knee flexed. Your weight shifts to the inside edge of your straighter outside leg as you feel pressure increase on that foot.

** The term "Commit" was suggested by Alan Bush, former Supervisor and Technical Director, Aspen Highland Ski School, Aspen, Colorado.*

To get more pressure on this leg, straighten the outside knee a little more or increase flexion of the inside knee. It is important to always maintain a little flexion in both knees so your knees never become totally straight. This preserves the option to extend your knee even more when you wish to apply a little more pressure. The inside leg should have very little pressure on it but keeping a little there will help it stay on track. (See Figure 17, banking by extending knee of outside leg more than inside leg, page 41).

The third element in the pure carved turn is initiating the turn with a little knee action, down-UP (or flexion-extension). The first two movements, inward lean and outside leg extension, are more important. But to smooth the transition between turns and to mark the end of one turn and the beginning of another, begin each turn with a quick, short flexion and extension of the knees. When extending, extend the outside knee more than the inside knee and you will immediately feel the shift in weight and pressure to the outside foot.

Timing is important. Some speed and momentum are essential before you can begin a turn with upper body lean because you must generate centrifugal force to lean against. And, once you have momentum, you don't want to slow down too much or you lose the momentum and can't bank the next turn. Therefore, when using inward lean, you must maintain a continuous speed and rhythm with one turn flowing into the next without stopping.

To stress the importance of weight transfer to the turning ski, many skiers were taught to shift all of their weight to the outside ski and to pick up the heel of the inside ski to make sure the ski is under no pressure. However, 100% weight on the turning ski is not essential for recreational skiing. I like to keep a little weight on my inside ski to keep it from wandering. Sliding the inside ski a few inches ahead of the outside ski will help keep the inside ski from crossing. In deep powder, there is little transferring of weight from foot to foot. Weight must remain distributed fairly evenly between the two feet to maintain balance. If you can ski with both feet weighted in powder you can certainly do it on packed snow, too.

Parallel turns with rotation

Pivoting your skis by rotating your feet, hips, shoulders, or arms is the other way to parallel turn. You have already discovered that twisting or rotating your shoulders and arms will pivot your skis in a new direction. To become a better skier you must learn to do your pivoting with your feet only. Shoulder rotation is the novice way to finish turns. As you improve, you will finish your turns using edge control without shoulder rotation, and you will initiate short radius turns with foot twists.

Pivoting both feet

The more difficult type of parallel turn is pivoting both feet in unison. The concept is easy for some skiers to grasp, difficult for others. Pivoting both feet can be visualized if you are seated with your feet off the ground, such as sitting on a chair lift. With your feet and skis suspended in air, bring your skis together and simultaneously twist them to one side and then the other keeping the two feet together all the time. Place your hands on your knees to keep them from pivoting too (See Figure 37, sitting on chair lift pivoting feet, page 81). The twisting action you do is rotation; rotating the skis by pivoting only your feet and lower legs. The upper body is fixed, not rotating at all.

Pressure release (Unweighting)

When skiing, your goal is to twist your feet simultaneously from side to side, just like you did on the chair lift. However, it's difficult to pivot your feet when your weight is on the ground. When there is pressure on them, the skis don't move when you twist your feet. Even rotating your shoulders may not get the skis to turn. Why? Obviously the answer is friction. The way to overcome it is to take your weight off your feet at the moment you want to pivot. If you can make your skis weightless for an instant, you can pivot your feet and skis easily, just as you did sitting on the chair lift.

For many intermediates, learning to release pressure from your feet to unweight your skis is the most difficult part of parallel turning. Once you conquer this, the rest is pretty easy and you are well on your way to becoming a better skier. Down-UP pressure release is the technic to start with; it's simply a hop up. But you can't hop up unless your knees are bent. The flexed knees give you the spring board from which to hop up. Hence, pressure release by hopping up is often called "down-UP pressure release" or unweighting. The down portion is to remind you to first flex your knees before you hop up.

The terms down-UP and flexion-extension of the knees have been used interchangeably. However, it is worth pointing out that "flexion" and "down" are not always the same movement. I prefer the term down because it gives you two desirable actions at once without realizing or thinking about it. "Down" means dropping your seat over your heels, something that is easy to do. By doing this, you must flex your knees and your ankles simultaneously. Just flexing your knees drops your weight back on your heels, which is not desirable. To counterbalance this backward transfer of weight, you should push your knees forward when flexing them. This is done by flexing your ankles forward. This is a lot to remember: Flex your knees and push them forward. This combination is simple to perform by simply dropping your seat over your heels, or dropping your seat "down". Dropping your seat down, then lifting it up, will give you the proper flexion and extension of both knees and ankles without focusing on technical jargon. On the other hand, if you are already into the terms flexion and extension use them in place of down-up. (See Figure 27, balance, page 62)

Ski poles are very helpful in learning to release pressure. By planting the pole just before you take the weight off your feet, the pole maintains your contact with the snow as your feet lose their contact with it. The pole acts as a stabilizer during the moment your feet are weightless.

Basic parallel turns

The basic parallel turn has 4 steps:

1. Down--drop your seat a few inches over

Basic elements of parallel turns *Figure 41*

1) The turn begins with down-UP pressure release to unweight. **2)** During the moment of pressure release, the feet rotate in the direction of the turn. **3)** Knee angulation completes the turn by controlling the edges of the skis as they either skid or carve.

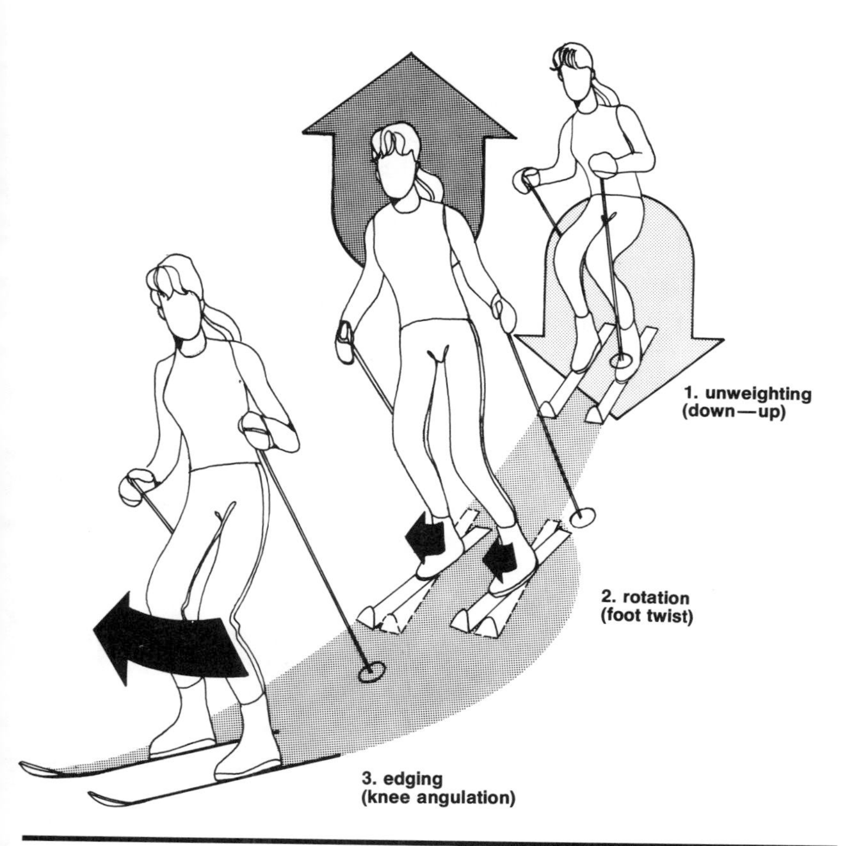

your heels (flex your knees and ankles)

2. Pole plant–use your wrist, plant a little ahead and to the side; don't reach with your arm
3. Up--quickly lift your seat (extend your knees)
4. Pivot--twist your feet in the new direction

This sequence, down, pole plant, up, and pivot represents the first half or the initiation of the turn. The turn is completed by angulating your knees into the hill and carving or skidding **[Figure 41]**.

Emphasis in the basic parallel turn is on the actions of the knees. First, the knees flex to lower your seat. In practice, its helpful to exaggerate this, dropping the seat 4-6 inches. As you progress it is not necessary to drop your seat this far. The distance you drop your seat depends on how flexed your knees are when you start. Better skiers have their knees flexed a few inches most of the time. Therefore dropping down from an already flexed position requires lowering your seat only an inch or two.

Next, your knees perform the up action, by straightening or extending. You can lift your seat several inches although it is not necessary to lift up this much. An UP action of just an inch or two is enough, providing it is a quick lift up. Speed, not distance, is what counts. The faster you lift the more effective will be the pressure release.

Timing the foot pivot is critical. It must come at the moment of pressure release; the instant you lift up. Since the only purpose of releasing pressure is to provide an opportunity to pivot your feet when they are weightless, the pivot must be timed to occur at that moment; otherwise the down-UP action was wasted.

Timing the pole plant is also important. It must immediately precede the up motion. Since the purpose of the pole plant is to stabilize your body during the moment of weightlessness, it must be planted with the up motion or a split second before. You can perform your down motion ahead of time and hold it for a few seconds; there is no rush at this point to continue rapidly. However, once the pole is planted the up action must follow immediately or you will ski past the pole plant and have to release the pole before you've even started your turn.

Wedeln–get some rhythm

Once you've learned to release pressure, pole plant, and pivot, you can start to get rhythm into your skiing. Putting together a sequence of turns to a regular rhythm (wedeln) is one of your goals. To do this initially, ski on a gentle smooth slope, head straight down the fall line,

Simple Wedeln

Figure 42

In simple wedeln, the upper body remains facing downhill all the time so it is always in a position of anticipation. The down motion is followed immediately by the pole plant and the UP motion to release pressure. While unweighted, a quick foot twist and/or edge change occurs. The turn is finished with a minimal skid or carve, which is accompanied by the down motion for the next turn.

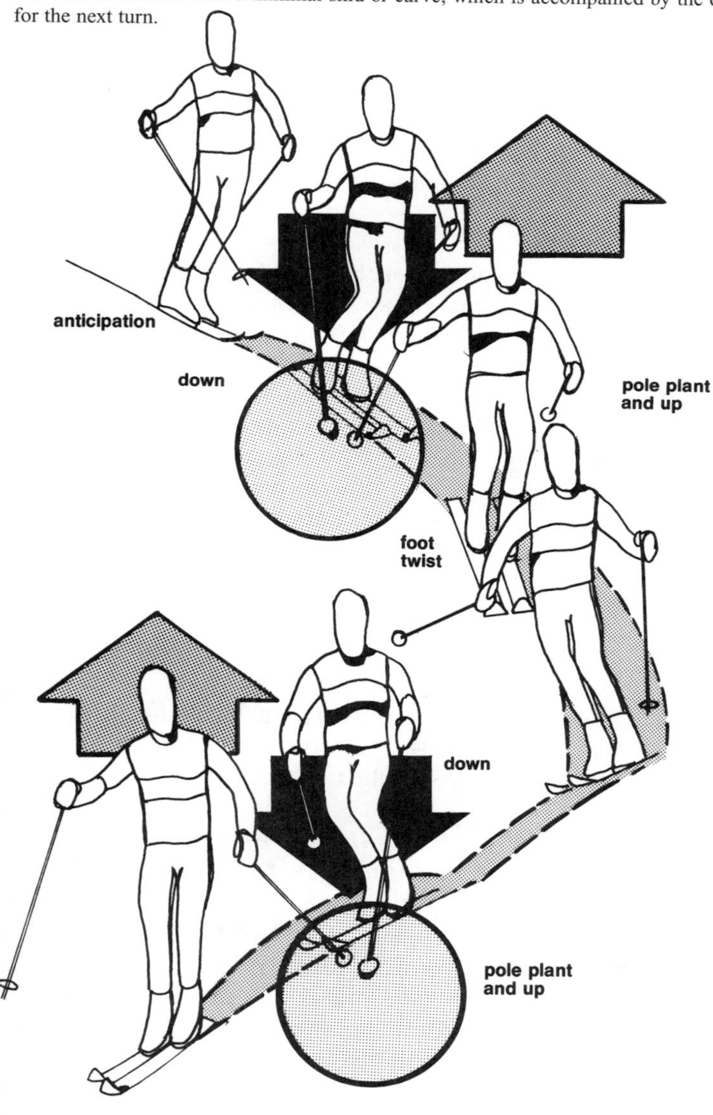

and practice just bending and straightening your knees at a slow pace. After several down-UPs, begin to add the pole plant just before the up action; then add the foot pivot during the up action. It will be rough and awkward at first, but concentrate on keeping the regular pattern of down-UP, down-UP to a steady slow rhythm. You don't have to pivot far, but your feet should be pivoting back and forth across the fall line **[Figure 42]**. If you are on a very gentle slope, even these little turns may be enough to control your speed. Finally, observe the good skiers wedeln down the slope around you; try to copy them.

Better parallel turns

After you've learned to release pressure, pole plant, and pivot, you can focus on some of the secondary issues in parallel turning. Mastering these points will permit you to ski difficult terrain with the same ease you ski gentle terrain. These include:

1. knee angulation to complete turns
2. dropping your seat down at the end of the turn, after crossing the fall line; this action to complete one turn is also the preliminary action for the beginning of the next turn
3. extra knee angulation (pre-turn) just before you pole plant
4. anticipation--shoulders facing downhill before the turn **[Figure 43]**
5. banking--leaning inward early in the turn
6. weight forward--pressing your shins into your boot tops early in the turn

Pre-turn or check—end of one turn is start of another

After lifting your seat and pivoting your feet, your skis usually have more turning or checking to do. This is done by bending your knees a little more and by angulating them into the hill. To slow down more, angulate your knees even further into the hill. This combination of movements, flexing and angulating your knees at the completion of a turn, is the same action that has been described as a pre-turn, the action that initiates the next turn. The use of the same movement to complete one turn

Parallel turn with anticipation *Figure 43*

From a traverse position, anticipate by facing your shoulders downhill. The down motion is followed by a pole plant which signals a quick lift up. While the feet are unweighted, they are twisted in the direction of the turn. In this example, the turn is being completed by carving.

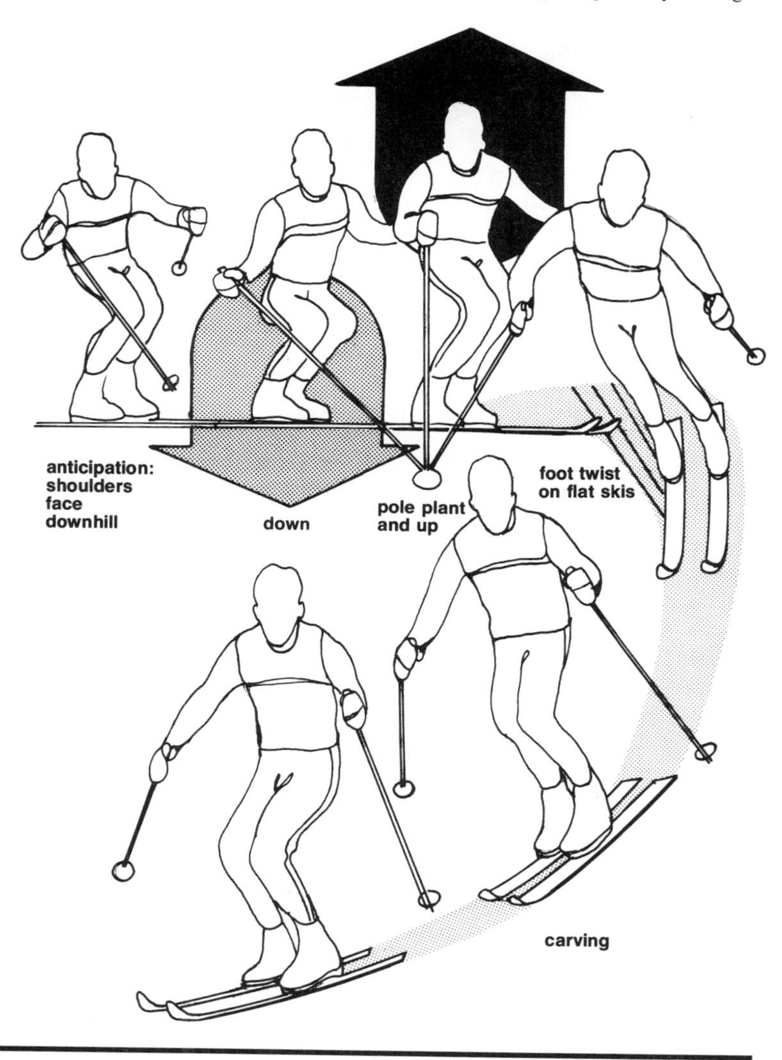

and simultaneously initiate another is what permits you to link your turns together in a nice rhythm. When this knee angulation is quick it produces a sudden **check** to reduce speed; when knee angulation is slower it results in a smoother **pre-turn** which also reduces speed, but not as much as the check.

Wedeln down a gentle slope is one of the best ways to practice this. The rhythm used to learn wedlin has four steps: 1) down, 2) pole plant, 3) up, and 4) foot twist. The addition of the pre-turn gives the new wedeln a fifth step that is added after the down action but before the pole plant. The new rhythm is: 1) down, 2) knee angulation to check or pre-turn, 3) pole plant, 4) up, and 5) foot twist **[Figure 44]**. The amount of knee angulation you use depends upon how much slowing you desire. If you wish to slow down a lot, push your knees harder into the hill and hold it a little longer than you would if you wanted just a little speed reduction.

Smoothing out your turns is achieved by **simultaneously** flexing and angulating your knees. Combining the two actions in a single movement softens the abruptness of first flexing then angulating your knees. This is the next step in progressing toward advanced skiing. This should also be practiced on a gentle, smooth slope. Wedeln now goes back to four steps because the first two, "down" and "knee angulation" are combined into one: 1) combined down and knee angulation, 2) pole plant, 3) up, and 4) foot twist.

Anticipation

Maintaining your shoulders and hips constantly facing downhill is one of the marks of an accomplished skier. As an intermediate, you probably feel the need to rotate your shoulders with the turn so your shoulders follow your ski tips. However, try to control your speed with knee angulation alone and keep your shoulders facing downhill, that is, hold the turning shoulder back so you feel your upper body trying to twist away from the direction your skis are pointing.

Its easier to learn anticipation on gentle slopes where you have more time to let knee angulation control your speed and you are less likely to need your shoulders to rotate through your turns for survival. By letting your

Pre-turn/checking

Figure 44

Wedeln with pre-turns and checks utilizes a prolonged sideslip and check before each turn. Begin with anticipation. The down motion is prolonged by angulating the knees uphill at the end of the down motion. This tightens the leg muscles as the lower body prepares to lift up. The pole is planted and the stretched leg muscles rebound by springing the body up. While pressure is released, the unweighted feet are easily twisted to face downhill and continue to turn across the fall line. In this example, the turn is completed by skidding.

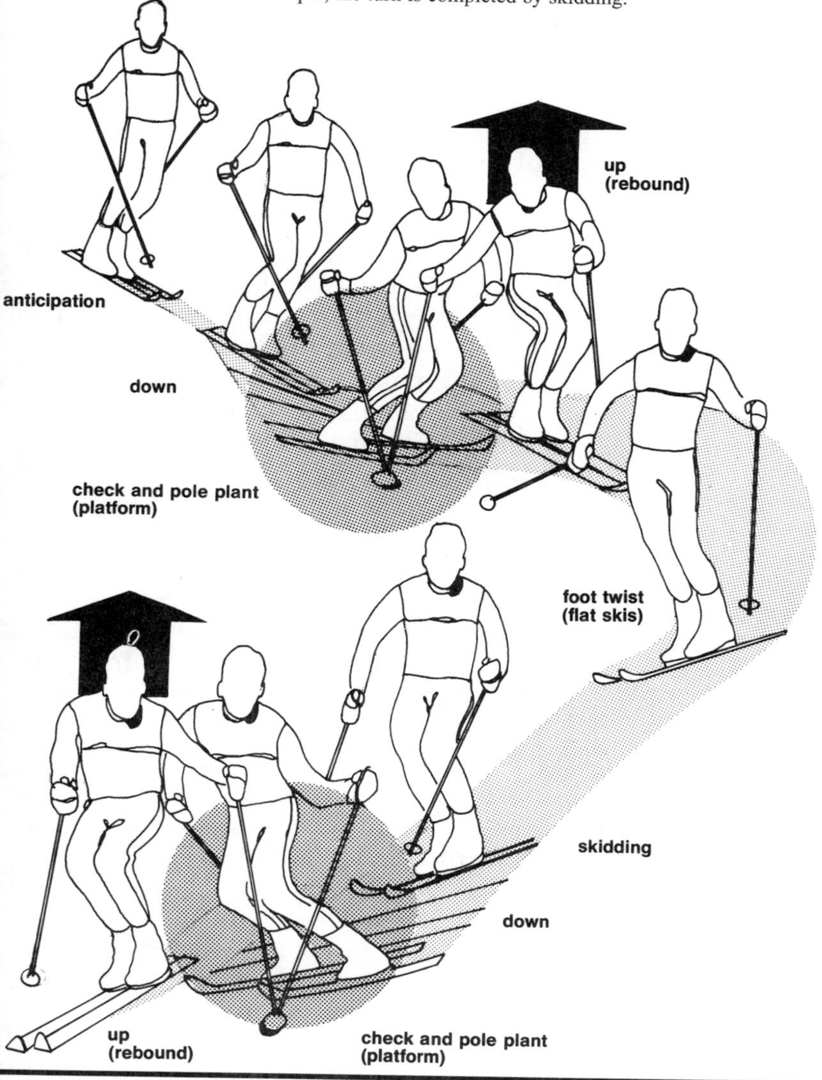

lower body do all the twisting from side to fall line, each time you release pressure your long body muscles will untwist automatically, starting the pivot of your skis in the new direction. Adding a little foot twist to the momentum already started is quite easy and is almost effortless. Your turns are quick, and most important, your upper body is always in position for the next turn. This lets you put together a sequence of fast turns in rapid succession. While it is possible to perform a sequence of turns with shoulder rotation too, this is much slower and requires more energy than keeping your shoulders always facing downhill.

Banking

Banking was discussed earlier in this chapter as a good technic for large radius turns. Banking is also an action that can be added in other situations to assist in edging your skis and taking strain off your knees, that is, reducing the need for strenuous knee angulation. Just as in wide arc turns banking begins when shifting weight to the turning ski, in short arc turns with foot twisting, banking is added at the beginning of the turn. The time to lean inward is immediately after the pole plant and simultaneously with the up motion. The inward direction of the upper body lean is toward the center of the turn, **and** downward, down the fall line. You should feel your shins pushing against your boot tops. The inward lean is achieved by your hips and upper body moving from one side to the other of the vertical line of your body.

Banking lets your ski edges switch from one side to the other and sets the opposite pair of edges quickly, early in the turn. This results in your spending very little time with your skis flat on the snow; you continuously crossover from one set of edges to the other. Because you are usually on your edges, you can be carving most of your turns, which gives you better speed control.

Banking requires a little extra time to perform than just lifting up and pivoting your feet. However, you can add banking to a wedeln rhythm by making it a little slower. The new sequence becomes 1) down and knee angulate, 2) pole plant, 3) up **and** inward lean, and 4) foot twist. This sequence will be very helpful on steeper slopes, but the best place to practice it is on a gentle one.

Combining skills

Combining anticipation with leaning the upper body inward is a common combination of skills employed by advanced skiers (sometimes referred to as dynamic anticipation). By twisting your upper body to keep your shoulders facing downhill and at the same time using inward and downward lean of your upper body to direct you into each turn, you start to ski with your entire body. The upper body is now taking some of the work load from your legs. You still must knee angulate and edge, but you don't have to push as hard or angulate as far because upper body banking is helping you edge. Your entire body weight is pressuring your edges so you don't have to push as hard with your knees.

Minor points

Weighting the uphill ski is something that is commonly taught to avoid. When learning to stem turn, instructors often emphasize the importance of weighting the turning ski by having you put all of your weight on that ski. However, this is done for instructional purposes and needn't be regarded as a rule for life.

For many years I tried to ski with all of my weight on the downhill ski. When I started to ski in deep powder, I had to learn to keep almost half my weight on the uphill ski. It was surprising to discover how much more relaxed it was. At about the same time, I became aware of my ski tips crossing many times in a run, particularly in moguls. Since this didn't happen in powder, I began to ski the bumps with weight on each ski. When the skis were facing straight down the fall line, the weight was about evenly distributed; when traversing, more was on the downhill ski, but a little was kept on the uphill ski. This worked well. By weighting the uphill ski, the ski stayed in its track better than when it was totally unweighted.

It was difficult at first to remember to weight the

uphill ski, having skied for so many years with all of my weight on one ski. To break this old habit and learn a new one, I began skiing gentle slopes with most of my weight on the uphill ski; that's right, the wrong ski. This worked. It is harder to keep your balance by putting all of your weight on the outside edge of the uphill ski; it feels like ice skating and is exactly what is done when skating on skis. However, having felt the independent action of the uphill ski, it became easier to ski with weight on both skis much of the time.

The conclusion from this comparison of weighting just the downhill ski versus both skis is that both technics can be effective. More important, the emphasis of putting 100% of your weight on the downhill ski is the wrong point of emphasis, particularly for recreational skiing. Keeping some weight on your uphill ski has several advantages: It's more comfortable; its easier to keep your balance; your ski tips are less apt to cross; and you don't have to concentrate on keeping all your weight on the downhill ski. In addition, you can ski powder and packed snow with the same technic. With weight evenly distributed between your two skis you sometimes can experience that wonderful sensation of being on a mono-ski as your two feet do everything in unison as if they were one.

There are times when it feels more comfortable to put all or most of your weight on one ski, particularly on smooth, gentle slopes. At other times, weighting both skis is more comfortable, particularly in difficult terrain. Try it both ways and use the technic that feels most comfortable at the time. There are no fixed rules.

Lifting your inside ski is stressed by some instructors as a technic to make sure you have 100% of your weight on the downhill ski. For racers this is important; it puts all of your weight on the turning ski to give it maximum carving ability and reduce skidding. The fraction of a second saved can mean the difference between first place and tenth place in some races. However, in recreational skiing seldom is "maximum" carving performance essential. More often your goal in a turn is to reduce speed rather than accelerate.

Advancing your uphill ski a couple of inches ahead of the downhill ski is a maneuver that helps keep your shoulders downhill. The more you traverse perpendicular to the fall line, the more important this is; the closer you are to skiing straight down the fall line, the less important.

Touching the knees together is a habit I have found helpful. While some instructors advise against this because it inhibits independent leg action, I seldom find it a problem. The advantage of locking the knees together is that it permits one leg to feel what the other is doing. Particularly when turning to a rapid rhythm, keeping the knees touching helps the skis turn simultaneously and reduces the tips crossing. Try skiing with your knees touching and with them a little apart. Use what feels most comfortable to you.

Leaning forward, pushing your shins against your boot tops, puts a little more weight on your tips which is helpful early in a turn. The tips of the skis hold the slope better than the tails which permits the tails to smoothly pivot faster than the tips (skidding) to give you tighter turns. Once you've turned enough, correct the forward lean by bringing some weight back to your heels. This puts more weight on your tails to stop the pivot and lets you carve the end of the turn. Thus, the completion phase of these turns is a combination of skidding early and carving late.

Leaning forward permits you to make a turn with a large change in direction. If you need only a small direction change, you don't need the forward lean. Just keep your weight centered with your tails and tips equally weighted to carve the entire completion phase.

Do not flex knees too early after the UP motion. Following your pole plant and UP-movement, do not begin the down motion for the completion of that turn until your skis have crossed the fall line. This will help you use that down action for the beginning of your next turn.

Chapter 11

Steep slopes

Short radius turns
Anticipation
Weight forward
Pole plants
Pre-turns and checking
Shoulders and skis in opposite directions
Compression
Foot thrust forward and jetting
Commitment
Difference between checking and pre-turns
Hip Angulation
Carving and skidding

Summary: Steep slopes require more skills than gentle ones. Rotation and pressure release technics must be developed to control your speed on steep pitches. It can't be done by edging and balance maneuvers alone.

All technics for steep slopes can be learned on gentle slopes. However many technics that are effective on gentle slopes will be ineffective on steep ones. A number of the methods for skiing steep slopes are discussed in the previous chapter. These can be practiced on gentle slopes until the mechanics and timing have been mastered; then try them on steeper terrain. If you can't properly perform a turning technic on a gentle slope, you certainly won't be able to do it on a steep one. For steep slopes, the technics to focus on are:

1. Strong knee angulation--to control speed with edges
2. Short radius turns--cross the fall line early
3. Pressure release (unweight) and foot twist-the best way to initiate short radius turns
4. Anticipation--shoulders and hips facing down hill all the time
5. Preturns and checking--roll knees uphill just

before initiating turn
6. Early banking--upper body lean to inside of turn at beginning of turn
7. Pole plants--with wrists and quick release
8. Lean downhill at beginning of turn

If you read Chapter 10: Gentle slopes, none of these points are new to you; they are some of the same ones. The difference is emphasis. On steep slopes you can't get away with the long radius turns you performed on gentle slopes because you will be going too fast to comfortably control your speed. (Of course, if you are a racer and are aspiring for speed, go with the long radius turns.) On steep slopes, speed control is a primary concern. Knowing how to stop by turning your skis across the hill and rolling your edges into the hill must be appreciated. Developing this skill is essential to mastering steep slopes.

Short radius turns

Do you find yourself skiing nicely on a gentle slope but suddenly find yourself going too fast for comfort when you enter a steeper pitch? Possibly you are using stem turns, shifting weight from one foot to the other **without** releasing pressure. Strong skiers can sometimes get away with this by using brute force, but it takes a lot of energy. Most skiers have trouble using the stem on steep slopes. Why?

Turns initiated with an edge change or stem movement are rather slow. The turn is completed by skidding until the tails of the skis have rotated past the fall line. Even though this takes only a few seconds, on steeper slopes you can develop considerable speed in those few seconds. Because the increased speed is faster than you desire, the natural tendency is to rotate your shoulders with the turn to slow down as quickly as possible. But now your shoulders are in line with the ski tips and face across the hill instead of down the fall line. Thus, you are unprepared for the next turn.

On steeper slopes, completing turns that start with edge change, requires you to angulate your knees **hard** into the hill to slow down by sideslipping or skidding before you can carve. This takes several seconds of time plus abundant strength to accomplish. It is hard to control the skid and most intermediates lose their momentum after each turn so a regular rhythm is never established. The stem turn which was so successful on gentle slopes is too exhausting and too uncontrollable on steeper terrain.

The primary difference in technique between gentle and steep slopes is in the first half of the turn, from the time you start the turn until your skis cross the fall line. On gentle slopes after your skis turn downhill, they usually have not accelerated very much before reaching the fall line, even with slow, long radius turns. In contrast, on steep slopes, a gradual initiation of a turn results in rapid acceleration before the fall line is reached. Thus, if the first half of your turn on a steep slope takes more than a second, you will be struggling in the second half to slow down.

The secret to conquering steep slopes is to initiate turns with a quick pivot of both feet so that your skis cross the fall line very early in the turn. The skis cross the fall line so quickly there is little time for them to accelerate at the beginning of the turn as happens with stem turns. The most efficient way of accomplishing the quick turn is to pressure release and pivot the skis rapidly.

Anticipation

Maintaining your hips and shoulders facing downhill **before** you initiate the turn is very important on steep slopes. If your shoulders are facing in the direction of your ski tips when you release pressure, it will take more time and much more energy to rotate your feet than if your shoulders are facing downhill **before** you release pressure by a down-UP movement.

Two other elements that assist short radius turns are: 1. leaning your body downhill at the start of the turn and 2. proper use of the pole plant. These points are not as important as releasing pressure and anticipating, but they become important as you strive to improve your parallel turns.

Weight forward

Weight forward is a common instruction, but one not easily defined. Weight forward at the beginning of a turn implies that your weight is in the center of your foot just prior to this moment. If your weight happens to be back on your heels, weight forward will mean leaning further forward than if your weight is centered. "Weight forward" carries two connotations: Forward towards your ski tips and forward down the fall line. If at the moment you lean forward your skis are heading straight downhill, these two forward leans are the same. If your skis are facing across the hill, weight forward usually means leaning towards your ski tips and a little down hill.

Forward pressure means increasing the pressure of your shins against your boot tops by pushing your knees forward, bending your ankles as far forward as they will go, but not by bending forward from the waist. The purpose of forward lean is to put more weight on your ski tips, helping them grab the snow, and less weight on your heels, making it easier and quicker for the ski tails to pivot around the tips. The purpose of forward lean **down the fall line** is to help you begin banking your skis early in the turn. The forward lean down the fall line is the same as leaning towards the inside of the turn, banking. In skiing, it is worthwhile leaning in both directions, forward and downhill, simultaneously; it accomplishes both goals with one motion.

Pole plants

As slopes get steeper pole plants become more important. You need more security and stability during the moment of pressure release on steeper pitches. The pole plant is the timing mechanism that makes you stay in rhythm. Once the pole is planted you are committed to proceed **now** with the lift and pivot. You can lean a **little** on the pole to assist you in releasing pressure, but do not rely heavily on it. Ideally, you shouldn't lean on it at all, but at times it is truly a nice "crutch" to lean on. Releasing the pole quickly also becomes more important. Pole plants were discussed in Chapter 9, but are worth reviewing here.

Keeping your arms and poles in front of you, particularly on steep slopes, helps keep your weight forward. There is a natural tendency on steeper slopes to keep your weight too far back toward your heels. The arms held forward counteract this tendency.

The pole should be planted with a flick of the wrist forward, and just a little arm motion. You don't want to disturb your balance with the pole plant and you don't want to lean too heavily on it. Plant the pole to the side of your foot, or a little in front of your foot. As you ski past the pole, push your wrist straight down the fall line, keeping your arm fixed in front of your body. As you move down the hill the pole should quickly come out of the snow. If you lean heavily on the pole, and if it stays in the snow too long, the pole holds your arm and shoulder back, rotating your shoulders uphill. This destroys your important goal of maintaining your shoulders facing downhill **all the time**, anticipating the next turn. (Of course if you are making long radius turns, it is not necessary to keep your shoulders facing downhill at all.)

Pre-turns and checking

Rolling the knees uphill (knee angulation) and increased knee flexion become increasingly important on steep slopes. On gentle slopes, you often don't need much braking when you wedel as the turn itself is a slowing action. On steep slopes this is not the case. The first action to maintain speed control on steep terrain is the short radius turn with a good lift up and pivot; the second action is a check or pre-turn. What you practiced on gentle slopes will now pay off on steep slopes. By making an extra roll of your knees and drop of your seat a routine part of the completion of each turn, you are building the preparation for the next turn (See Figure 44, page 113). Once you establish a rhythm of continuous actions in sequence, the momentum you have started at the end of one turn carries into the next turn. As this becomes an unremitting series of actions, you will find it hard to identify a precise beginning and ending of any turn.

Shoulders and skis in opposite directions

Constant asynchrony between upper and lower body is essential in controlling steep slopes. Keeping your shoulders and hips pointing down the fall line all the time is the beginning. With the completion of each turn, and as the pre-turn action commences, the lower body is turned further uphill and you should feel tightness developing in your long body muscles, especially in your belly. You can make these muscles a little tighter by twisting your upper body in the opposite direction of your skis at exactly the moment of the pre-turn. The extra twisting coils your long body muscles even tighter so that the moment you pole plant and lift, the long muscles recoil, untwist, and rapidly pivot your legs and skis automatically. Your skis should reach and cross the fall line so quickly that there has not been time for much acceleration.

Compression

As the pre-turn is completed, just before the pole is planted, your leg muscles are often extremely tight. They are at their maximum stretching point by the combination of knee flexion and knee angulation. The extra flexion of the knees, tucking your heels up under your seat, feels like you are trying to squeeze your lower body into a tight space. The term **compression** has been used to describe this compact feeling. The leg muscles are tightly compressed. The compression is augmented by the extra twist of the upper body described in the previous paragraph. At the moment the pole is planted, your leg muscles relax and the legs uncoil. The result is "rebounding" which can lift your body upwards or advance your feet forward. The upward movement releases pressure from your feet; the forward foot movement moves your weight backward toward your heels.

Thus, **compression** of the legs provides automatic rebound and pressure release; and **anticipation** provides automatic pivoting of the skis. Incorporating these elements into your skiing armamentarium is a major step in progressing from intermediate to advanced skiing.

Foot thrust forward and jetting

One of the subtle moves of advanced skiers is to thrust their feet forward during some turns. Pushing your feet forward, while the rest of your body is stationary, results in transferring some weight backward from your toes toward your heels. The pressure of your shins against your boot tops is relieved. The result is the opposite of leaning forward. Leaning forward weighted your ski tips to permit the tails of your skis to rotate faster around the tips creating a fast skid. In contrast, pushing your feet forward deters or prevents skidding so that the weight on your skis is more evenly distributed between tips and tails making carving easier.

Advancing your feet forward is another technic to smooth out your skiing. It can be applied anywhere in a turn. Thrusting your feet forward in the middle of a turn stops skidding and assists carving the completion of the turn.

Thrusting your feet forward at the beginning of a turn can be done by using the rebound from compression. After a check or preturn, as you plant your pole and begin to release pressure by rebounding up, keep your shoulders down to prevent your body from raising up. By relaxing your legs, your feet will automatically project forward. The rebound from compression has been redirected; your legs rebound forward instead of your whole body upward. The turn now begins by combining the forward advance of your feet with inward lean by your upper body. Your skis roll onto their edges and begin to carve at the beginning of the turn. This is a method of performing the complete carved turn. This is used more on gentle slopes than on steep ones because steep slopes usually need short radius initiations to turns. Advancing the feet forward, automatically, has been described as jetting (by Georges Joubert) **[Figure 45]**.

Commitment

Once you add the extra twist and tightness in your body during your pre-turn, you have stored up rotational energy that will carry you through the next turn. However, you should immediately proceed into the next turn or lose

Figure 45

Compression/jetting

Turns with compression and jetting (jet turns) begin with anticipation. Knee flexion (the down motion) and knee angulation occur together. This action compresses the lower body by tightening the leg muscles. The pole is planted and UP-pressure release follows. But instead of rebounding straight up as in check-wedlin, the legs relax and the upper body is prevented from rising up. The rebounding force is thereby diverted to push the knees upward and jet the feet forward. Only then do the feet pivot into the turn and face downhill. The slight delay in the foot twist results in the upper body's leaning inward, in a position for banking.

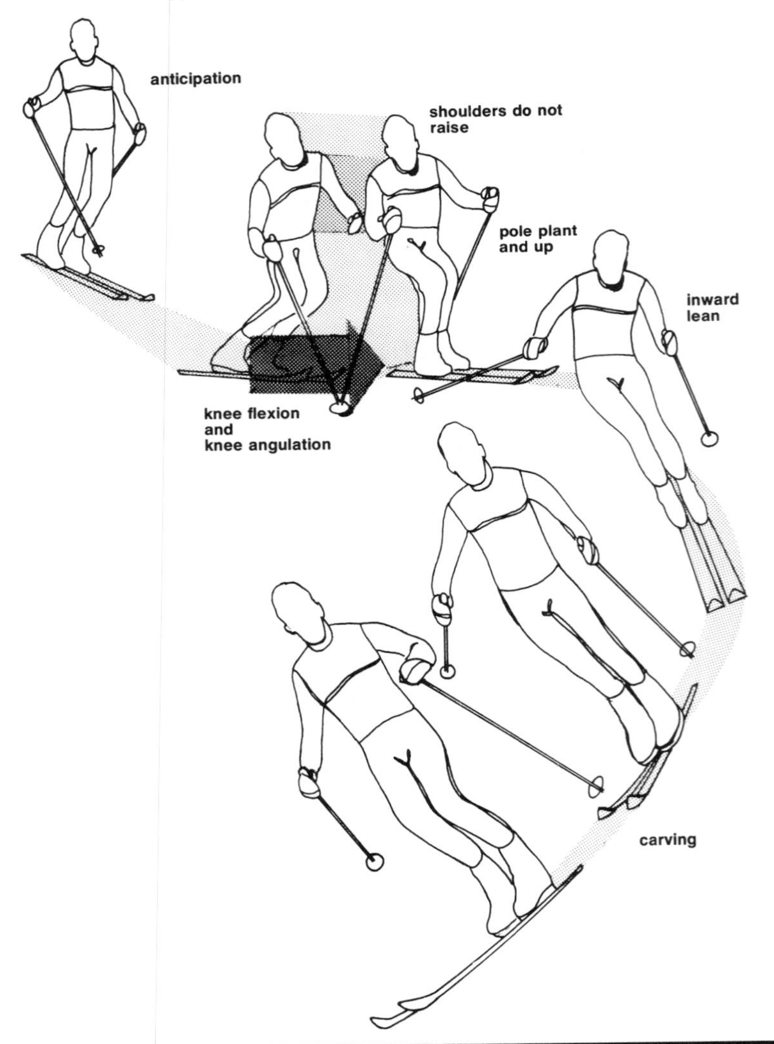

the built up energy. Those who hesitate are lost. Once you're compressed, delaying converts an easy turn into a more difficult one. Once you've begun, you're committed to finish what you've started. Even when you don't feel you're quite ready to turn, you should try to turn anyway.

Skiing to a regular rhythm is a mark of a good skier. Advanced skiers commit themselves to a regular rhythm which they try to maintain. The body quickly adjusts to the rhythm and it's usually best to try to stay with the rhythm as long as possible. When skiing with continuous turns straight down the fall line, your turns are too close together to mentally tell yourself each step of each turn. If you ski to a regular rhythm, your body learns to feel it and automatically responds with the proper sequence of actions at the correct time. Varying the rhythm alters your timing and it takes a few more turns for your body to adjust to a new rhythm.

Difference between checking and pre-turn

Checking is a quick, sudden action while a pre-turn is a slower, graceful turn of the skis uphill. Checking is more abrupt and faster; pre-turning is smoother and takes a little more time. A quick check will cut your speed instantly; the compression at the end of the check sets you up immediately for the next turn. With pre-turns it takes more time to slow down and to start the next turn. Checking allows you to turn rapidly; to perform turns in fewer seconds than pre-turning.

Checking can be performed in very narrow passages; pre-turning needs more space. Checking must be used on very steep terrain and in narrow chutes where pre-turns are too slow and require more room. Checking results in using more energy and tiring out sooner than with pre-turns. In general, I prefer pre-turns whenever it is possible to use them. However, in very difficult terrain and challenging conditions checking is the best method of speed control. Advanced skiers know how to perform both and use them appropriately.

Hip angulation

On steep slopes you often need all the edging you can

get. To attain extra edging and increase your braking action, hip angulation can be added to knee angulation. In this book, I have stressed the importance of knee angulation throughout and put little emphasis on hip angulation. The reason for this is that knee angulation is a far more versatile and rapid method of edge control than hip angulation. Most intermediates use hip angulation early in their ski experiences while few use knee angulation properly. Knee angulation, with all its variations, is a key to advanced skiing.

Having recognized knee angulation, the role of hip angulation should not be overlooked. Unless you are turning very rapidly, the extra time it takes to add hip angulation to knee angulation is worthwhile. It increases the degree of edging attainable and can help reduce the stress on your legs and knee joints that knee angulation produces.

Carving and skidding

Carving and skidding are the only two ways turns are completed. This is true on steep slopes as well as gentle ones. While following the tip of a carved ski is the ideal way to ski, carving produces only a long radius turn. This is fine on gentle slopes but generates too much speed on steep ones. On steep slopes carving is not used much. Pivoting the skis with a quick lift initiates the turns while skidding is needed for completion. If you are in a rhythm of continuous quick turns there is little room for carving.

Skidding, which combines sideslipping with rotation of the tails around the tips, becomes a necessity as slopes get steeper. On very steep slopes, once you lift and pivot, your edges will sideslip as you complete the turn. To continue turning your skis further uphill, put your weight forward by pushing your knees forward so you feel more pressure of your shins against the boot tops. But don't overturn so you come to a stop; don't lose your momentum. When you've slowed down enough, let your weight come back to the middle of your foot, increasing the weight on your tails and stopping the pivot. At this point in the turn, you have a choice of quickly setting your edges into the slope by checking with a rapid edge set or

Figure 46

Skidding

Skidding is completing a turn by sideslipping while the skis continue to rotate. The side of the ski leads the way through the turn, which leaves a wide track. Knee angulation controls the amount of edging needed to skid. On gentle slopes, the skies may lie flat against the hill , with no edging. On steep slopes edging is needed to control the skid. In this example, minimal edging is needed so no knee angulation is seen.

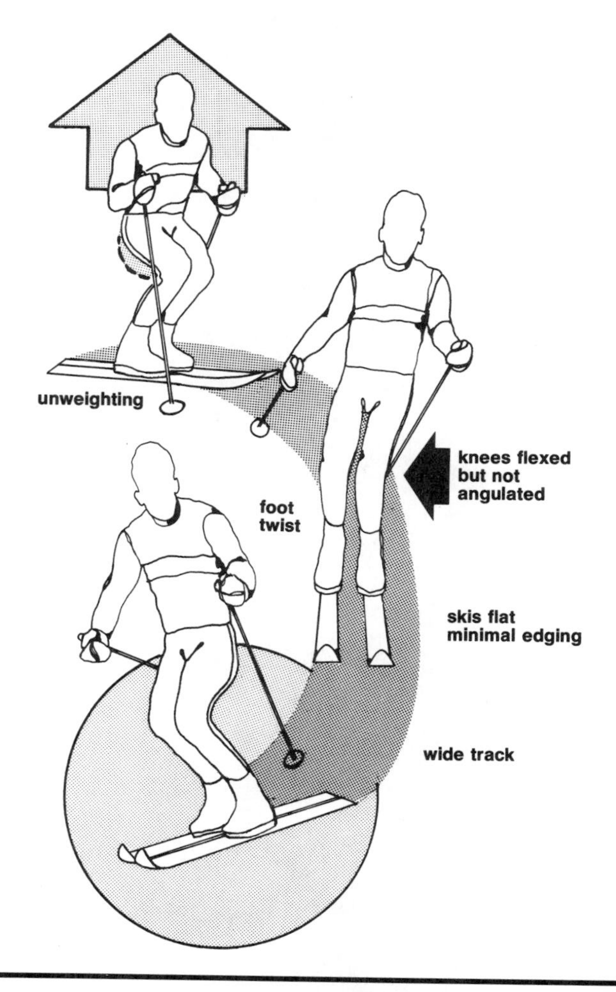

pre-turning with a smooth action that combines knee angulation and down motion. In either case, you immediately proceed into your next turn. If the slope is narrow

Carving

Figure 47

Carving is completing a turn by following the direction of the curve in the edged skis. The tips of the skis lead the turn, which produces a narrower track than a skidded turn. The skis are edged either by knee angulation, as shown here, or by banking. Realistically, most carved turns contain an element of skidding. It is almost impossible to carve without a little lateral slippage. In practice, carved turns are those with minimal lateral slippage.

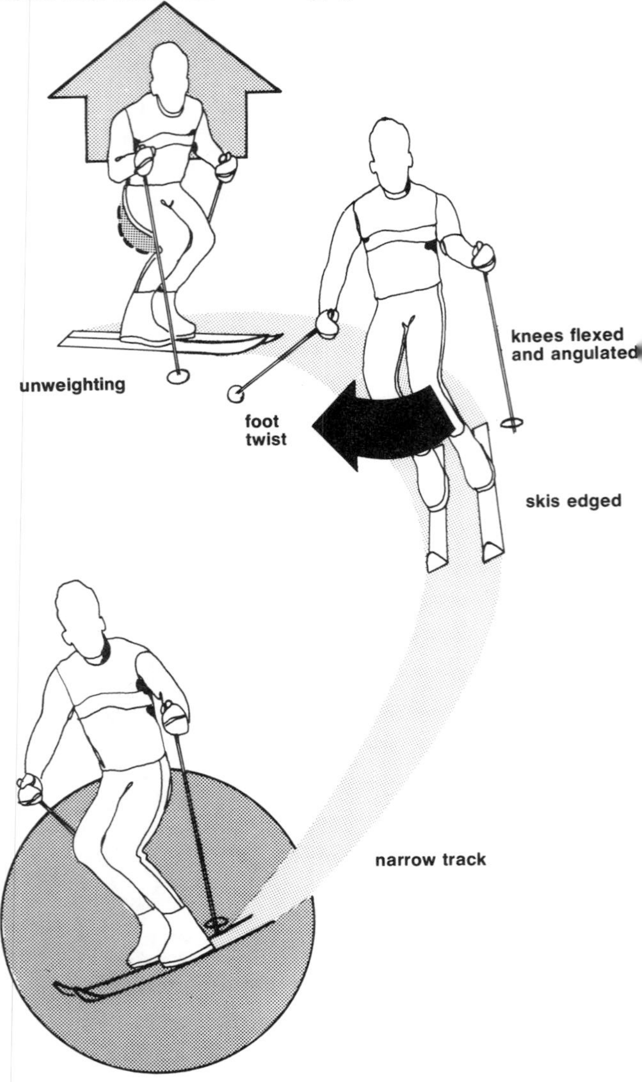

and you have a good rhythm going, you will check and go into the next turn **[Figures 46 and 47]**.

Carving is the smoothest and most comfortable way to complete a turn. In pure carving, the skis move forward, following their tips without sideslipping or skidding. The steeper the slope, the harder it is to avoid some skidding. Most turns are completed by a combination of skidding and carving. However, once the skidding and sideslipping have brought the skis around in the new direction and your speed is under control, continue immediately into the next turn with a check or pre-turn, pole plant, and lift.

Chapter 12

Bumps

Even pressure on your skis
Forward/backward balance
Pressure control
    Down-pressure release
    Turning on crest of a mogul
    Leg retraction
Differentiate down-unweighting from leg retraction
Routes and paths
    Ski troughs vs. avoid troughs
    Ski the banks
    Ski the mogul crests
Don't forget to breathe
Moguls on gentle vs. steep slopes
Pole plants
Anticipation

Summary: Moguls add a new challenge to the skier who already knows the basic skills of edging, balancing, rotation, and pressure control. In mogul fields, you must react quickly to changes in balance and alterations in the pressure against your skis. To ski moguls down the fall line you must be able to quickly release pressure, pivot your feet, and reapply pressure to avoid rapid acceleration and skiing out of control. The skills needed in moguls are the same skills you learned on gentle and steep slopes, but they must be applied differently.

Mogul fields are the major fear and frustration of intermediate skiers. While you can handle smooth slopes pretty well, and even steep slopes if they're smooth, things seem to fall apart in the moguls. As you turn on the crest of a steep mogul and begin to descend its back, your skis accelerate. You can't slow down and you begin to traverse. But the traverse is over more moguls which throw you backward and forward so quickly you can't gain your balance long enough to make a turn. What is going on?

Moguls are one of the toughest challenges in skiing. Before trying moguls you should be able to control your speed fairly well and make reasonably sharp turns on gentle smooth slopes. In moguls you not only must check and turn well but another two dimensions are added: Stability and balance. Moguls constantly toss you in the air and throw you off balance. You must learn to do all the things you've learned on smooth slopes **AND** learn to do them under adverse conditions.

Good mogul skiing requires establishing a turning rhythm that is usually much faster than the rhythm used on smooth slopes. In moguls you must turn more frequently and more quickly than on smooth slopes; sometimes you must turn before you're ready to turn. When this happens on a smooth slope you just ride out the turn until you're ready to turn again. If you try this in mogul fields, riding out the previous turn results in traversing across troughs and more moguls. You become more off balance and no better prepared to turn than you were before.

Moguls affect your skiing in several ways: They constantly alter the pressure of the slope against your skis; they challenge your ability to maintain your forward/backward balance; and the valleys between bumps can trap your skis in ruts which inhibit your turning.

Even pressure on your skis

Observing advanced skiers in moguls you may notice that as they ascend a mogul they bend their knees and as they descend a mogul they straighten them. Sometimes the movements are subtle but they are there. The purpose of this flexion and extension as you go up and down a mogul is to maintain even pressure of the slope against your skis.

Why is even pressure important? It gives you stability and confidence to control your speed. Pressure comes from the weight on your feet. When there is no weight on your feet, turning your skis on their edges has no effect. An edge with no weight on it accomplishes nothing.

As you descend a mogul, the resistance of the slope is moving away from your skis so there is very little of your weight exerting pressure on the snow. The extreme of no pressure at all under your feet is experienced by skiing over a jump where there is nothing beneath you. Once you are airborne, you have lost control because there is no weight under your feet. As a result, there is no way in which to edge and check your speed.

In principle, skiing the backside of a mogul is similar to the airborne skier. Your ski edges are only effective if they have weight on them and since they are carrying very little weight at that moment, they can't dig into the slope to slow you down. The solution to this is to get more weight on your feet, to get more pressure on your skis, by extending your knees as you start down the backside of the bump. In order to be able to extend your legs (straightening your knees) your knees must be flexed as you come over the crest of the mogul. However, if you are skiing moguls correctly, they will be flexed.

Just as pressure against your feet is reduced as you go down a mogul, the opposite occurs as you go up a mogul. Pressure against your feet increases as you ascend a mogul. To maintain even pressure as you ascend a bump, you drop your seat by flexing your knees. This lightens your feet as it is a form of pressure release (unweighting). Knee flexion keeps even pressure against your feet as you go up a mogul and positions you correctly to descend that mogul. As you descend, your legs are flexed at the start, so you have the necessary preparation to extend your legs as you descend the mogul.

If you have not felt this before, you can feel it by traversing a mogul field, flexing your knees as you go up the mogul and extending them as you go down it **[Figure 48]**.

Forward/backward balance

In addition to altering pressure beneath your feet, as you ascend a mogul your weight is thrown backward, putting more weight on your heels. This alters your forward-backward balance. As you reach the crest of the mogul, if your weight is too far back on your heels, it is more difficult to turn. Therefore, as you ascend the mogul, main-

Figure 48 **Absorbing bumps**

Going up a bump, bend (flex) your knees; and going down a bump, straighten them out (extend them). This maintains an even pressure of the skis against the slope. In addition, lean slightly forward when ascending and slightly backward when descending the bump.

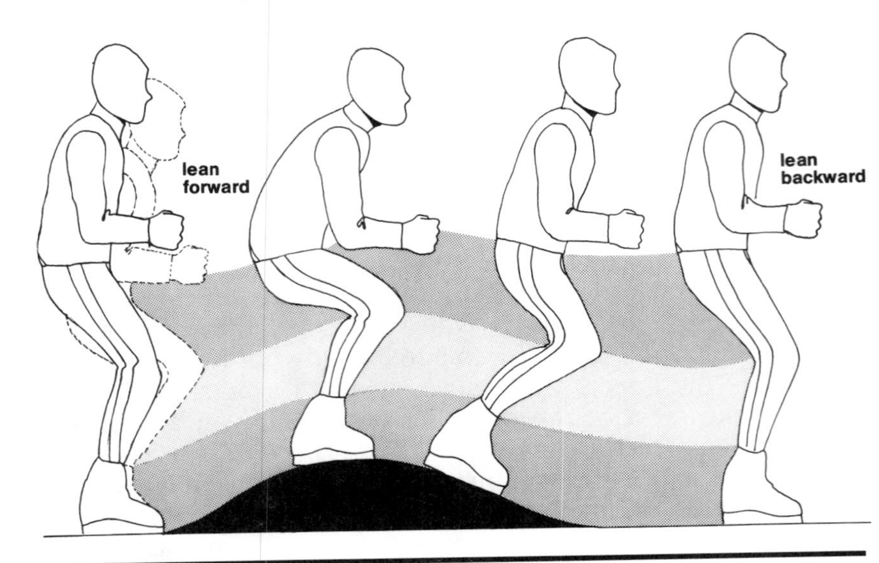

tain your balance by leaning forward, either with more flexion of your ankles or your waist. This is subtle; it doesn't take a lot of weight shift; you must feel your way. Your goal is to distribute your weight partly on your heels and partly with your shins pushing against your boot tops. For most skiers, the balance problem in moguls is having too much weight on your heels. You should always feel some pressure of your shins against your boot tops as you ascend as well as descend a mogul.

Putting some weight forward as you ascend a mogul can be done in only two ways: Increasing ankle flexion or bending forward at the waist. The choice is not arbitrary. Forward weight shift should always be done first with ankle flexion. This means pushing your shins and knees forward so you feel the pressure of the front of your leg against the tongue of your boot. The boot's stiffness limits the amount of forward weight shift possible. Knee flexion, dropping your seat, increases the weight on your heels, counter-balancing ankle flexion. These two must work together to keep your weight centered in the middle of your foot.

The simplest rule of thumb for proper forward/backward balance is to flex your knees by dropping your seat directly over your heels. When doing this, knee flexion and ankle flexion automatically move in tandem. However, after a moderate amount of knee flexion, the accompanying ankle flexion will reach a maximum because the ankles are not capable of as many degrees of flexion as the knees. From a standing position, the ankles can only flex forward about 45 degrees; the knees can flex over 90 degrees. When dropping your seat over your heels, you reach a point where the ankles can flex no further but the knees can. As the knees continue to flex, your seat begins to move behind your heels which moves the center of your body weight back, onto your heels and away from your toes. You notice that your shin can no longer press against the boot top. At this point, when the ankles are maximally flexed, forward balance is maintained by bending forward at the waist. However, waist flexion should not be used until ankle flexion is at its maximum (See Chapter 6: Balance).

When going up a mogul, maintain forward balance first by increasing ankle flexion. When you can flex your ankles no further and still feel your weight moving backwards, adjust this with waist flexion.

Pressure control

A major difference between skiing moguls and smooth slopes is the need for a variety of ways to release and apply pressure in mogul fields. On smooth slopes you can manage pretty well with basic down-UP-unweighting. However, in moguls it's helpful, and sometimes vital, to have additional ways to release pressure. In moguls you frequently wish to turn on a precise spot and you have no time to prepare. It takes several split seconds to go down-UP, and this may be too long; you've already passed the turning spot. The solution is to have a quicker way to release pressure.

Moguls provide one of the best ways to learn other

Figure 49 **Down-pressure release on a mogul**

To Down-pressure release, stand on top of a mogul with your skis facing across the hill. Begin by facing your shoulders downhill (anticipation). Next, plant your downhill pole 12 to 18 inches below your boot. As the body begins to tilt forward, suddenly and quicky flex your knees and drop your seat. Your feet will be pulled downhill into the turn. Complete the turn by skidding, carving, or both (steering). During completion, slowly extend your legs.

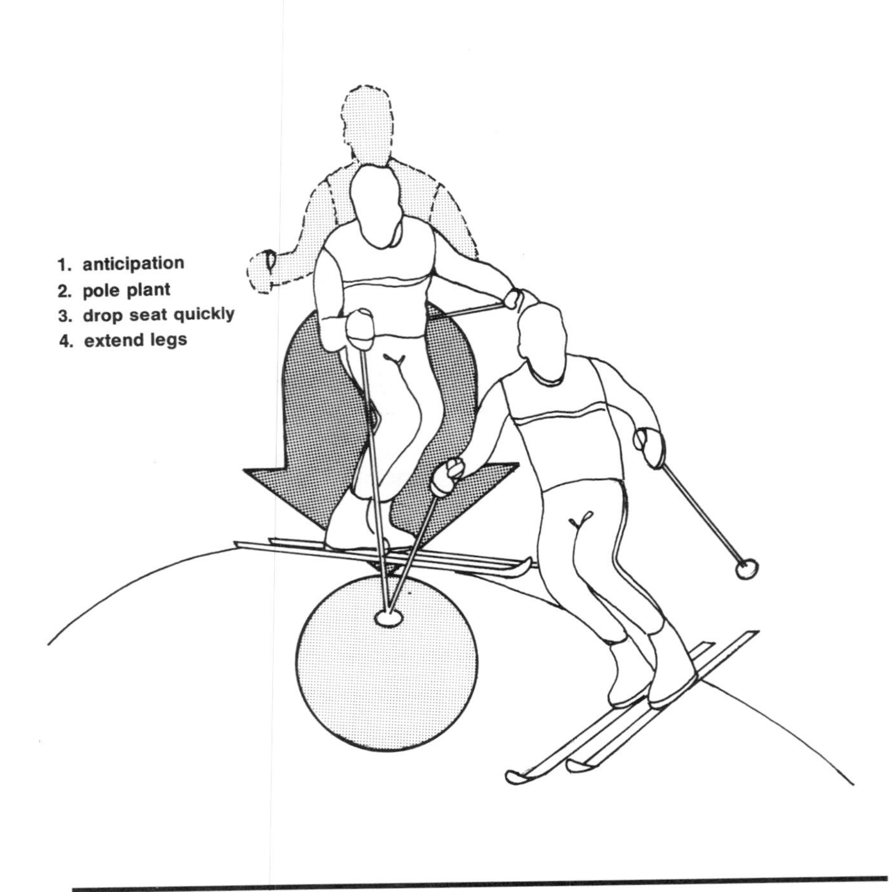

ways to release pressure--to provide that moment of time when the skis can pivot with little effort. The other methods of pressure release besides UP-unweighting are Down-unweighting, going over a mogul, and leg retraction.

Down-pressure release: The simple act of squatting, flexing your knees by dropping your seat, will reduce the weight on your feet momentarily. You can prove this to yourself by standing on a bathroom scale and watching the weight indicator as you drop your seat. The quicker you squat, the faster is the weight reduction. Each time you flex your knees while skiing you experience some pressure release from your feet. In fact, when you drop your seat as you complete a turn, you are partially unweighting your feet which makes it easier to steer your skis uphill to finish the turn.

Pressure release by dropping your weight down (Down-unweighting) is a convenient way to turn on some moguls, particularly if you have reached the crest of a mogul with your knees straight instead of flexed. There are only two steps in Down-unweighting: 1. Pole plant and 2. Down; there is no preliminary or preparatory action. As your feet lighten, pivot them across the fall line. Just as in down-UP-unweighting, maintaining your shoulders and hips facing downhill (anticipation) will start your feet pivoting automatically the moment you release pressure. If your shoulders are facing in the direction of your ski tips instead of downhill, it will take more time to turn. Leaning a little on your pole further lightens your feet, but don't leave the pole in the snow too long.

You can experience the feeling of Down-pressure release by standing still on the crest of a large, steep mogul. Point your skis perpendicular to the fall line; twist your shoulders and hips to face down the fall line so you feel your belly muscles tighten. Touch your pole straight downhill with your wrist 12 to18 inches directly below your heel. Now you're ready to Down-pressure release. Quickly, very quickly, drop your seat over your heels and simultaneously plunge your upper body straight down the fall line **[Figure 49]**. Place a little weight on your pole as you do this and push the pole forward with your wrist as you come through the turn. Don't worry, you won't fall over on your face.

Your skis should pivot across the fall line without gaining much speed. Keep your knees flexed until you

Figure 50

Pressure release over a mogul

From a traverse, begin by ascending a mogul in a fairly upright position. Anticipate by facing your shoulders downhill. Flex your knees slowly as you approach the crest. Plant the pole at the crest when the body is in a tucked position. As the skis pass the crest they automatically release pressure. Immediately twist your feet and slowly extend your legs to maintain pressure against the downside of the mogul to prevent speed acceleration.

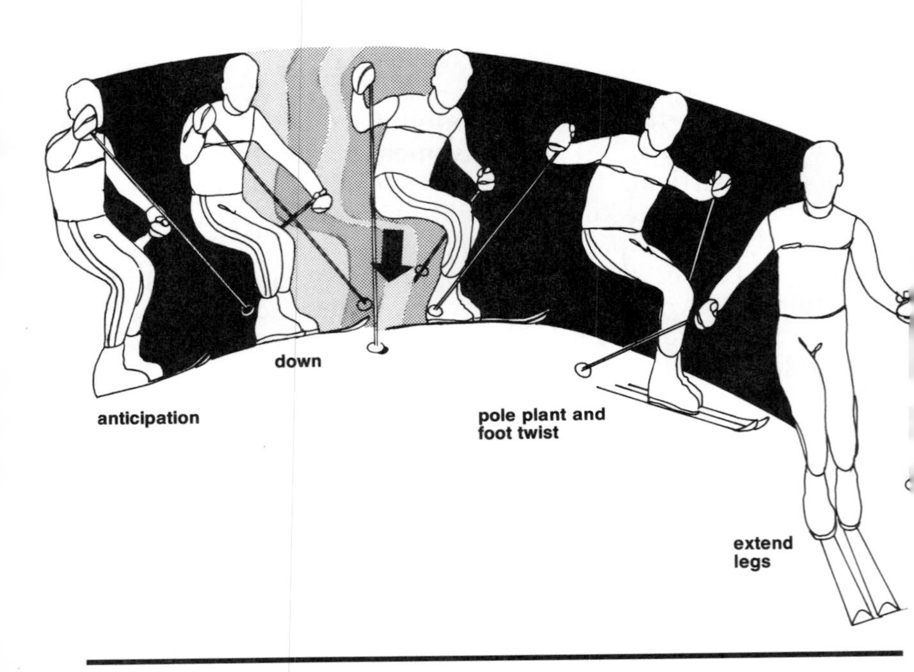

start down the crest of the mogul and then slowly extend your legs while angulating your knees uphill. It is this last action, straightening and angulating your knees, that increases the pressure on your skis, digs your edges into the hill, and thus controls your speed within a short distance **[Figure 50]**.

The two hardest elements of this exercise are: 1) dropping your seat quickly and 2) letting your body aggressively plunge straight down the fall line as you begin to release pressure Down-unweighting. This takes some practice. Initially it's hard to quickly drop your seat, but concentration will let you do it. Letting your body **fall straight down the fall line** is even harder to do at first. You must develop the courage and faith that as you begin to plunge downhill your legs will keep your skis beneath you. Actually, the more completely you can let your upper body drop downhill the faster will be your turn and the quicker will you be able to control your speed.

Incidently, the same exercise can be performed on a mogul with down-UP pressure release to unweight. Start by standing still on a mogul crest with your knees flexed several inches instead of straight. Your skis are facing across the hill and shoulders facing downhill. Plant your pole below your heel, drop your seat, and quickly lift your seat, just a couple of inches, so that your knees are still quite flexed as you release pressure. You should feel as if you are picking up your heels beneath your seat. Your feet will automatically pivot as you start down the mogul. Since you've kept your knees flexed, you can extend your legs to increase edging pressure as you complete the turn.

Letting your upper body plunge down the fall line is also helpful when UP-unweighting as well as Down-unweighting. If your fear is too great to let yourself go straight down the fall line on a steep mogul, begin this exercise with a mogul on a gentle slope.

Like steep smooth slopes, skiing on steep moguls requires short radius turns initiated with a quick action. Your goal is to cross the fall line before your skis can accelerate, then check your speed and proceed immediately into the next turn. Ideally, the next turn should occur on the down side of the same mogul upon whose crest you just finished turning.

Turning on crest of a mogul: The easiest way to release pressure is by simply skiing over the crest of a sharp mogul. At the moment your feet pass the peak of the mogul, your ski tips and tails are suspended in air (See Figure 35, pressure release on a mogul, page 77). Your feet are partially unweighted as you begin down the mogul. At this instant you can pivot your feet or simply shift weight from your downhill to your uphill ski. Either way, pivoting or transferring weight from foot to foot, you will produce an easy turn, although a longer radius turn.

This is a passive way to release pressure, that is, you do not have to actively lift or drop your weight; the terrain actually does the work for you. However, this type of pressure release does not allow quick, big pivots that can turn 180 degrees. It will work with small moguls, and moguls on gentle slopes, but it may not be as effective on steep moguls. On steep moguls you need a bigger pivot, the kind you can only produce with active pressure release.

Leg retraction: The quickest, most efficient, and most difficult way to release pressure is by leg retracting. This is also the smoothest way. It is performed from a knee flexed position by quickly tensing your abdominal muscles and simultaneously lifting your knees upwards. This is a form of UP-unweighting. Because lifting your knees up tends to throw your weight back, leg retracting should be accompanied by a short, quick flex of the waist forward to keep your forward/backward balance.

The advantage of leg retraction is it permits you to release pressure expeditiously, with almost imperceptible vertical motion. Preparation by the upper body is by isometric contraction of abdominal muscles which is quicker than either down or up actions.

Pressure release occurs by increasing knee flexion with a quick action that is followed, almost immediately, by automatic extension of the legs when the muscle tension is released. By leg retracting on top of a mogul, the automatic extension occurs on the down side of the mogul, just when you want it to occur to help you increase pressure and edge your skis as you complete the turn. The speed of this whole action lets you complete turns rapidly so you can turn again on the same mogul if you wish (See Chapter 7: Pressure control, Figures 30 and 31, pages 72 and 73).

Differentiate Down-unweighting from leg retraction

It is important to recognize the difference between Down-unweighting and leg retraction. When Down-unweighting you drop your seat, flexing your knees quickly. It is the **quick flexing** of your knees that releases pressure and unweights you. When leg retracting, knee flexion is a preliminary action, not the main pressure release action. The pressure release comes from tightening your abdominal muscles and **lifting** your knees. Leg retraction is a form of UP-unweighting.

Leg retraction from a knee-extended position, that is with your knees straight, requires that you first drop your seat a few inches in preparation for leg retracting. If you flex your knees quickly and then leg retract, you will experience a combination of pressure release by both Down-unweighting **and** leg retracting. If you slowly flex your knees you will not get much pressure release from the down action. If you are staying constantly in a knee-flexed position you get no pressure release from the down position, but you will be able to turn faster and have a quicker sequence of your turns by quick leg retractions from the maintained knee flexed position.

Routes and paths

It sounds good to plan a route down a mogul field, deciding at the start just where you will make each turn. However, I have never been able to carry out my plan. Usually, I can only plan two or three turns ahead. After that, the next turn comes when you've completed the previous one, and you can't be sure precisely where that will be. A momentary loss of balance, a patch of ice, or numerous other things can delay a given turn; you must be prepared to handle it and then proceed on, wherever you may be at that moment. In general, your goal is to ski as close to the fall line as possible and avoid traversing as much as possible. You should either be initiating a turn or completing one, rarely coasting or traversing between turns.

How you ski a given mogul field depends upon how quickly you can lift and pivot, check your speed, and turn again. Your path on gentle mogul fields may be much closer to the fall line than on steep, large mogul fields. Speed control and maintaining balance are the big challenges in bumps.

You do not have to use the same technic of unweighting for every turn. Vary them. Letting the mogul unweight you gives you a gentle, slower turn than Down-unweighting or leg retracting. UP-unweighting, particularly when preceded by a check, gives you more time to pivot and slow down. If you find yourself tiring after making a series of quick turns in moguls, slow down a bit by checking hard and UP-unweighting a few turns. This will let you regain your composure.

Skiing troughs vs. avoiding troughs: The contours of the valleys between mogul crests vary greatly. They may be gentle "U" shaped, or they may be very abrupt "V" shaped. The gentle valleys with wide troughs and gradual ascending sides usually present few problems and you can ski across them or in them with impunity. If you ski in the gentle valleys you can usually turn where you wish without the skis being trapped in the valley. One way to ski moguls is to just remain in the troughs turning quickly with the trough line. When doing this you cannot easily check so that skiing the troughs is usually limited to gentle slopes.

In steep, "V" shaped valleys, if you begin to ski in the valley, you may have trouble getting out of the tight grooves. Furthermore, these valleys seldom permit you to edge your skis for braking purposes. As a result, if you are caught in one of these troughs, you may find yourself accelerating and unable to slow down quickly.

To avoid being limited by the troughs, try not to get into these "V" shaped narrow troughs. Plan your turns to cross them perpendicular to the line of the trough. If you do get stuck in a trough, you may get out of it by letting your skis ride up onto one side of the trough by banking your body with the turn.

Ski the banks: Another route to follow is up the sides of the moguls, banking your body from one side to the other as your skis cross the trough and ascend the opposite side. Banking, leaning your entire body to the inside of your turn, permits the contour of the slope to help you turn. Your skis remain flat against the snow and you do not have to angulate your knees too hard to control speed. This can give you a little rest and conserve some energy.

Ski the mogul crests: The mogul route I like best is directly up and over the peak of as many moguls as possible. Ascending the ridge of a mogul will slow you down because the uphill position of the mogul is a built-in braking mechanism. Increase knee flexion as you ascend the mogul. At the crest, release pressure by either a quick lift up, a quick down motion, or by leg retracting. Pivot both feet at the moment of pressure release. Regardless of how you release pressure, your knees should remain flexed. The turn is fast, with your lower body pivoting and your upper body remaining facing downhill. There should be no shoulder rotation. The direction change is completed in just a few feet.

After pivoting, quickly proceed to either pre-turn or check and immediately perform another turn on the backside of the mogul. Approaching the valley, try to ski across it rather than getting your skis trapped in it. If the valley is shallow, you can make your next turn in it and move straight up the ridge of the next mogul. However, if you have to cross over the next valley, the succeeding turn depends on where you are after crossing the trough. You may have to ski on the side of the mogul if you aren't in good position to turn straight up its ridge.

This all sounds easy on paper. However, it is only possible if you can totally control your speed with your knees alone. Shoulders and hips must remain facing downhill all the time. If you rotate your shoulders to help complete your turn, you will not be ready soon enough for the next turn on the downside ridge of the mogul.

Don't forget to breathe

A common pitfall when skiing difficult moguls is to hold your breath. It happens without thinking about it. After making several quick turns in succession, you may sometimes find yourself gasping for breath. If this is happening to you, try concentrating on breathing as you descend the moguls. You may be holding your breath without realizing it.

Moguls on gentle vs. steep slopes

Whether the slope is smooth or bumpy, gentle pitches are always easier to ski than steep ones. On gentle slopes with moguls, there is less acceleration on the downside of the bump so you don't have to angulate your knees as hard at the end of the turn. Checking or pre-turning may not be necessary if your speed is slow enough. Turns can be just 20^0-30^0 from the fall line instead of 50^0-60^0 as on some steep slopes. It is much easier to ski the fall line on gentle slopes.

Steep slopes with moguls require a pre-turn or check to reduce speed before each turn just as on steep smooth slopes. Because there is not much room and not much time to perform the pre-turn, checking is more frequently used in steep moguls; it's faster. On gentle slopes several types of pressure release can be used effectively. However, on steep slopes the best way is probably UP-unweighting with a big pivot leading immediately into a check and another UP-unweight. I have found that leg retraction and Down-unweighting in steep moguls don't permit as big a pivot as basic UP-unweighting. On steep moguls, you can perform a few turns with other methods of pressure release, but your speed accelerates too quickly. To slow down and regain good control of your speed, yet still maintain a reasonable rhythm, try a few turns with UP-unweighting, big pivots, and big changes of direction.

Pole plants

On moguls, pole plants are more important than on smooth slopes. On smooth slopes I often find it unnecessary to use my poles at all, especially on gentle smooth slopes. In bumps it's different. The pole becomes an important and necessary stabilizer on gentle as well as steep moguls because the bumps themselves tend to throw you off balance.

The principles of pole planting in moguls are the same as on smooth slopes. Arms and poles should be held in front and to the side of your body all the time; the pole is planted to the side with the wrist and is released quickly by pushing the wrist forward, down the fall line; the arms should always remain in front of your body. Do not try to reach forward with your arm to plant your pole. This will rotate your shoulders in the wrong direction, reducing the turning force of your tightened long body muscles. However, you can advance your pole forward with your wrist. Immediately after planting the pole, let your body plunge down the fall line as well as lean forward, feeling your shins push against your boot tops.

Anticipation

During the pre-turn or check, your shoulders remain facing downhill; you feel you are twisting your shoulders in the opposite direction of your skis. As you feel the tightening of your long body muscles, plant your pole and simultaneously release pressure with a quick down-UP motion. Keep your feet on the ground so edging to reduce speed can begin immediately after the pivot. Flexing your knees on the way up the mogul so they can be straightened on the way down will help increase weight on your edges to more effectively bite the downside of the hill after the turn.

Chapter 13
Powder

Pack vs. powder
Shallow vs. deep powder
Equipment
- *Flexibility*
- *Binding position*
- *Wide skis*
- *Ski length*

Getting started in deep powder
- *Rhythm*
- *Pivoting in powder*
- *Knee angulation*

Subtle points
- *Foot advance*
- *Flexion-extension or compression turns*
- *Banking*

3 rules of powder
- *Weight equal on both feet*
- *Weight centered, not too much forward*
- *Complete turns by carving*

Steepness of slope
- *Gentle slopes*
- *Steep slopes*

Summary: Skiing on deep powder snow is more like floating on water than resting on a firm base. There are three rules of deep powder skiing: 1) Turns must be completed by carving, not skidding; 2) There must never be more weight on your toes than your heels; and 3) both feet should be equally weighted.

Pack vs. powder

The major difference between packed and powder snow is the contact between you and the snow. On packed slopes the only contact and resistance to movement is through the ski resting on the snow; the only braking action is the friction between the bottom of the ski and the packed snow, which isn't much. In contrast, shallow powder pushes against your boot and deep powder pushes against your lower leg. The powder supplies resistance to forward and sideways movement and acts as a constant brake to slow you down, more so than the friction between the bottom of the ski and snow.

Another feature of powder, and the one I like most, is its reliability and consistency; powder provides a much more dependable base than hardpack for setting your edges to carve or brake. One of the concerns when skiing on hardpack is that your edges may skid or slide when you want them to hold; you don't always have the edge control you would like. Unfortunately, you can't be sure when your edges will fail, therefore, you must always ski hardpack with a little caution and reserve. This is most evident on icy slopes.

In powder you don't have to worry about your edges holding. In powder, you don't need sharp edges; even the dullest edges handle beautifully. The reason is that in powder you don't use edges at all. On packed snow rolling your knees to the side sets your skis on their edges, so only the edges contact the snow. The bottoms of the skis are in the air. In powder the same leg action, rolling your knees, has an entirely different effect on the skis. The bottoms of the skis are always contacting the snow, whether the skis lie flat or are tilted on their sides. In powder, rolling your knees to the side banks the skis in the same way water skis are banked. Distributing your weight over the entire surface of both skis in powder is more secure and more stable than carrying your weight on the inside edges of one or both skis as you do on packed snow. As a result, in powder you can relax, roll your knees to the side, and immediately feel the gentle resistance of soft snow as it is packed below the entire bottoms of your skis.

The consistency and depth of powder is an important factor in the amount of resistance there is to turning. Very light, dry powder offers so little resistance that skiing through it is almost like skiing on a packed slope. Heavy powder, on the other hand, offers greater resistance to movement; it slows you down quickly but makes it much more difficult to turn.

One of the biggest differences between pack and powder is that in deep powder sideslipping and skidding are difficult to impossible to perform. If you are a skier accustomed to controlling your speed by skidding and sideslipping at the end of a turn, powder can be a nightmare. This is often the primary reason many intermediate skiers have trouble with deep powder: Skidding won't work. Turns must be completed by following the tip of the ski, carving (see below, 3 rules of powder).

Shallow vs deep powder

Very shallow powder, one to two inches, provides the best of pack and powder: The shallow snow is a good base for reliable, dependable edging; its thin layer permits you to turn just as you would on hard pack without experiencing the resistance of deep powder to turning.

Shallow powder, a few inches deep, offers resistance to forward and sideways movement of the ski, but the ski still lies on a firm base. The tip and tail of the ski can still grab the base when the ski is angulated to carve.

Deep powder, over 18 inches or 45 cm deep, is a new sensation. You are almost floating; the skis are resting on softly packed snow with no firm base beneath them. If too much weight is transferred forward, toward the tips, the skis can dive deeper causing you to fall forward, digging your head into the snow (called a "face plant"). To avoid this, many people are instructed to keep their "weight back in powder".

However, putting all or most of your weight back on you heels in powder is also a mistake. You can’t control your turns and you exhaust the energy in your thighs if you ski with your weight on your heels in powder (or, for that matter, on hard packed slopes, too). In powder, as on pack, you should strive to maintain some of your weight

Figure 51 **Position in Powder**

Knee flexion and ankle flexion combine to keep the weight balanced across your feet. In the proper stance you should feel the pressure of your shins against your boot tops and also some weight on your heels. How much weight? Just enough to keep your ski tips pointing towards the surface of the snow.

pushing against the top of your boot. You should feel your shin pressing against the tongue of your boot throughout each turn, as well as a little weight on your heels **[Figure 51]**. How then do you avoid diving over the tips of your skis if your weight is forward? The answer is by proper equipment selection and correct binding mounting.

Equipment in powder

A good powder ski is one that is very flexible, is wider

Stiff vs flexible ski *Figure 52*

Top) In deep snow, a stiff ski distributes your weight fairly evenly throughout the ski. Only a minimal curve is formed in the ski. **Bottom)** The flexible ski keeps more of your weight in the center of the ski. This produces a greater curve. When the skis are rolled onto their edges, this arc will be followed to carve turns in powder.

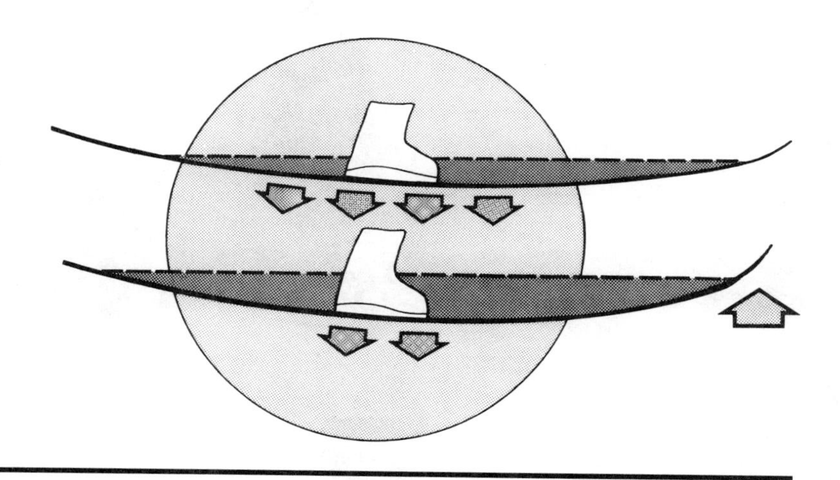

than the normal ski, and has the bindings mounted so that your weight lies a little behind the center of the ski.

Flexibility is the most important feature. In deep powder, your weight makes the skis sink into the snow until the packed snow beneath the skis drops no further. The depth the ski sinks is directly dependent on the amount of weight on the ski. There may still be another several feet of loose snow beneath your packed tract, but your skis will stay "floating" on the snow just as a piece of wood floats on water.

A stiff ski sinks into the snow with the entire length of the ski dropping to the same depth. The line of a stiff ski in deep powder is straight, with the ski's tip, tail, and waist all the same depth below the surface. If just slightly more of your body weight shifts forward, the ski tip dives deeper and you fall, face first, over your tips. However, with a flexible ski the center of the ski, that part directly under your foot, sinks the deepest while the tip and tail are not as deep because there is less weight over

Figure 53 **Stiff vs. flexible board**

Top) The stiff board distributes weight fairly evenly across the board so no arc develops. **Bottom)** The flexible board carries most of the weight in the center, less weight at the ends. The resulting curve is a marked contrast from the stiff board.

them **[Figure 52]**. The result is a curved ski with the tip and tail closer to the surface than the mid-section. On such a ski, there is leeway to put more weight forward yet still maintain adequate forward/backward balance. The tip of a flexible ski can hold quite a bit of weight before it dives deeper to produce a head plant.

A ski resting on powder is similar to a board resting on a mattress. If a person stands in the center of the board, the board will sink a few inches into the mattress. **[Figure 53]**. If the board is stiff it will sink fairly evenly into the mattress, maintaining a straight line. However, if the board is flexible, the center of the board (under the feet) will sink deeper than the ends of the board, producing an arc.

Binding position: The point on the ski where your foot is placed is more important in powder than on pack. For packed slopes, the binding is usually mounted so the tip of your boot is about 1 cm in front of the mid-point of the ski. This puts more weight on the tip to assist turning on packed slopes, when your weight is in the center of the ski. On pack, the weighted ski tip grabs the snow while the tail pivots around the tip. In powder, if the binding is ahead of the middle of the ski, the tip of the ski already has increased weight when your weight is centered. If you now transfer some weight forward by pushing your shins against your boot tops, you may get too much weight forward and make your tips dive too deep. To avoid this you must put your weight back, towards your heels, making turning difficult and balancing very strenuous on your legs.

The solution to easier and better balance in powder is to mount the binding a little further back from the standard position recommended by the manufacturer. A move of only 1-2 cm is usually plenty. This permits you to stand comfortably on the ski with your weight in the center of your foot. You can then exert considerable forward pressure on the ski tips without the tips diving too deep. **CAUTION**: When using this ski on packed snow, the tip will not bite the snow to perform skidded turns as well as a ski with a more forward mounted binding. There is no ski mounting that is ideal for all conditions.

Wide skis: On packed snow, the width of a ski is important for ease of edging. A narrow ski is easier to angulate and set on its edge than a wide ski. While this is also true in powder, another factor comes into play: The deeper the ski sinks into powder, the greater the resistance to turning. In powder, a narrower ski sinks deeper than a wide ski because the greater the surface area under your foot, the closer to the surface your ski rides. If the ski is very wide, it will float nearer the surface than a thin ski. For this reason, it is easier to turn and control a wide ski in powder compared to a narrow ski; and the wider the ski the greater the control. Particularly in difficult conditions such as heavy moist snow, wind-blown or sun-baked crust, broken tracts, loose snow, or corn snow, the wider ski is more stable, holds its line better, and feels more secure than narrower skis. Because very wide skis lie closer to the surface, skiing on them makes skiing in deep powder almost as easy as skiing in shallow powder.

Ski length: Powder increases resistance to turning; so does a longer ski. In deep snow riding a shorter length ski than you use on packed slopes makes skiing easier, particularly when skiing powder in tight trees. The effects of combining powder and length are cumulative. The deeper and heavier the powder and the longer the ski, the more difficult it is to turn and the greater the energy requirement. While you can't control the conditions of the powder, you can control the length of your skis; shorter skis are easier in difficult snow.

The advantage of length is greater stability at higher speeds. In deep powder, you usually ski slower than normal. However, in any long powder run, the snow conditions vary throughout the run. The powder may be light and shallow above tree line, get heavier in the trees, then thin out again at lower elevations. By selecting shorter length skis for the more difficult conditions, you may have to accept some instability in the lighter powder where you tend to ski faster.

The ideal ski: Is there a ski that is ideal in all snow conditions? No. Many skiers who do a lot of skiing have more than one pair of skis. A longer, stiffer ski is better for cruising, especially at faster speeds. In powder, a ski that is wider, shorter, and more flexible, with the binding mounted a little further back than usual, will perform better. In bumps, a flexible, shorter ski, especially with flexion in the tip, is desirable. If you wish to use just one ski for all conditions, I prefer a flexible ski that can be used in bumps and powder reasonably well and accept the slight chatter and instability that occurs in such a ski at cruising speeds. The binding position is a compromise between the ideal for pack and powder.

Getting started in deep powder

If you haven't yet learned down-UP pressure release, this is the time to start. If you are very strong, you might be able to power your way through powder with stem turns or by shifting weight from one ski to the other; but there are easier ways. To master powder, you must learn down-UP pressure release. Next, while unweighted, you must pivot your feet. Finally, you must complete your turn by rolling your knees in the direction of the turn, carving.

Rhythm & down-UP pressure release

A regular down-UP rhythm is the place to begin in powder. The principle is exactly the same as described in Chapter 10: Gentle slopes, under "Wedeln, get some rhythm". However, in powder, the rhythm is slower than on packed snow. One of the pleasures of deep powder skiing is that the entire rhythm of skiing can be done in slow motion. When learning to handle powder, exaggerate your pressure release, slowly going down and forcefully lifting your seat up. Exaggeration is the key–drop your seat several inches down, lift it several inches up. But don't totally straighten your knees; always maintain a little flexion.

Get a little speed before trying to turn. In starting from a standstill, point your skis straight down the fall line and begin slowly going down-UP, down-UP, etc., until you have generated some momentum. It is harder to pivot your skis in powder than on pack; it is even harder when moving slowly. Don't start pivoting until you have some speed and momentum.

Poles and arms are very helpful in powder, particularly for balance. Exaggerating the pole and arm action is also helpful, especially when making your first turns in a run. In addition to planting one pole, try simultaneously lifting the other pole. Lift the arm high, at least to shoulder level; it helps raise and unweight your whole body. Begin the arm action along with the bouncing up and down for a few cycles even though you haven't started turning. The arms alternate with each UP movement of your lower body. This helps you establish a comfortable rhythm.

While exaggerated pressure release and arm action is not essential in powder skiing, it is an excellent technic to have among your skills. When beginning a run in very deep or very heavy powder, many experienced powder skiers will employ these exaggerated actions to help start a good rhythm.

Pivoting in powder

A good rhythm and developing a good bounce is just the first step in managing deep powder. Two other elements must be added to turn effectively: pivoting and knee angulating. On gentle and moderate slopes you don't have to pivot your feet very far, a little pivot is usually enough. On gentle slopes, you often don't have to pivot at all. However, to control your speed in deep powder on moderate and steep slopes, you must pivot your skis across the fall line early in the turn, just as on steep slopes. But in powder, this is more important than on pack. On pack, if you accelerate too much in initiating your turn, you can cut your speed by skidding the end of the turn. But in deep powder, it is much more difficult to skid; your skis won't sideslip easily, so you must either carve the completion of the turn or fall.

However, even though skidding is difficult in deep powder, pivoting at the beginning of the turn can usually be done IF you release pressure and use your rotation power properly. This at least means pivoting your feet, and depending on how heavy and resistant the powder is, you may also need anticipation, shoulder rotation, and at times even hip rotation. Use whatever it takes to pivot your skis quickly at the beginning of the turn to avoid acceleration here.

Knee angulation in powder

Knee angulation is essential to complete each turn. I recall the comment a friend made when I was first learning to ski powder. After coming down a moderately steep slope with a good bouncing rhythm but a little too fast, he told me to look at my track in the snow. It was a straight line; it had none of the gentle curves that denote a good powder track. It was this observation that focused my attention on how to achieve the smooth series of arcs that distinguish the powder skier. The answer is simple: Knee angulation.

In powder, it is essential to complete your turns by rolling the skis on their sides, primarily with knee angulation **[Figure 54]**. Simply roll your knees to the side and begin dropping your seat as you complete the turn. A little steering action can be used at this point. Steering is combining knee angulation and twisting your feet in the direction of your turn plus feeling your shins push against your boot tops. Finish the turn by knee angulating gradually, as you lower your seat in the next down motion for the succeeding turn.

Just as on packed slopes when learning to wedel, emphasize the rhythm. Even if your turn is not fully completed, try to develop a continuous, regular rhythm by beginning the next turn on time. But remember, in powder the rhythm is slower than on pack. You must have enough time for knee angulation to turn you past the fall line. Eventually, if you are lifting your weight from both feet and flexing and angulating your knees slowly at the end of each turn, you will start to feel the control and smoothness of powder skiing.

Subtle points

Foot advance: One more element can be added to the turn once you've learned to pivot and knee angulate. Just after you've lifted and as you begin to angulate your knees and drop your seat to complete the turn, slide your feet a little forward, ahead of the rest of your body. This maneuver straightens your ankles and pulls your shins away from your boot tops for a short interval. It transfers some weight to your heels in the completion phase of the turn which helps smooth out the turn. As you begin your next turn, flex both your knees and ankles to get your weight back forward and again feel your shins push against your boot tops.

Sliding your feet forward is not an essential element. It is employed on gentle and moderate slopes only, not on steep slopes. Its purpose is to reduce the tendency to over-

Figure 54 **Knee angulation to complete turns in powder**

To complete turns in powder, roll your knees to the side, keeping weight on both feet.

turn by carving too far from the fall line. On steep slopes you usually want all of the turn you can get, so don't slide your feet forward on very steep pitches.

Flexion-extension or compression turns: Leg retraction can be used to release pressure in powder just as it is used on moguls or packed slopes. Since in powder it is desirable to maintain a knee-flexed position most of the time, tightening your abdominal muscles and lifting your knees up is an alternative way to release pressure. Leg retracting is quicker and smoother. Lifting your knees shifts your weight back toward your heels so you must compensate for this by flexing your waist to move your upper body forward. This combination of pulling your knees up and bending your chest down produces a tight, tense body position referred to as compression because the body is compressed into a ball. Once compressed the feet pivot; you then simply relax your leg and belly muscles. The result is a quick decompression. The upper body and knees automatically rebound by extending the legs and lifting the chest. This occurs rapidly and permits you to make a sequence of fast turns.

Slower, long radius turns can also be made with this "compression" technic. After the legs automatically extend, partially straightening your knees, you can actively extend your legs, straightening your knees further as you smoothly carve the end of your turn. The next turn is started by flexing your knees (dropping your seat), then leg retracting, rebounding, and slowly extending your knees again. Flexing, retracting, and extending in this way can be done to a rapid, slow, or very slow rhythm. This feels similar to skiing in bumps, tucking your legs up as you ascend a mogul and extending them as you descend.

However, there are limits to leg retraction. Because it provides only a short moment of unweighting, leg retraction works best in soft powder where the skis pivot easily and short angled turns are adequate. If the snow is heavy and difficult to move, down-UP pressure release gives you more time and a better opportunity to generate more turning power to cut through the powder. Down-UP pressure release also permits more time to accomplish large angle turns, close to 180^0. Thus, down-UP pressure release can be used for all snow and slope conditions and in changing snow while compression turns are limited to better snow on slopes that aren't too steep.

Banking: Just as on packed snow, leaning your upper body towards the center of a turn can be used in powder. However, when banking in deep powder with your skis "floating" in the snow it is not necessary to extend the outside ski more than the inside ski. In deep powder, the resistance to the skis is on the entire bottom of the skis, not just the edges, so that both skis equally share your weight in powder.

Three rules of powder

The practical question in powder is: Does the skiing technic in powder differ from the technic on packed slopes? Usually the answer is yes. Although it is possible to successfully use powder technics on packed slopes, most skiers modify their technics for different snow conditions.

Three significant technical points are essential for good powder skiing. I call them the "Three Rules of Powder". They are not required on packed slopes, but are essential to ski powder well.

1. Both feet equally weighted
2. Weight balance not too far forward
3. Complete turns by carving, not skidding

While these are technics especially for powder skiing, all powder technics can be learned on packed slopes. As a matter of fact, you can use powder technics on packed slopes all the time. If you learn them on pack, you won't have to change technics in powder.

1. Equal weight on both feet: A ski sinks in powder to a depth directly related to the amount of weight on that ski. If all of your weight is carried on one ski and none on the other, the weighted ski will sink many inches into the snow while the unweighted ski will stay on the surface. The result is skiing with your skis on two different levels which is awkward and uncomfortable and leads to imbalance, crossing ski tips, and difficult control. To avoid this, your skis should be equally weighted in powder so both skis sink to the same level. The skis should remain equally weighted through each turn although some inequality doesn't matter. When traversing on a steep slope more weight will fall onto the downhill ski. It is fine to leave it there.

2. Weight centered, not too far forward: As

pointed out earlier in this chapter, the forward/backward weight distribution is much more important in powder than on packed snow. Putting too much weight forward, on the front of your foot, can make the ski tips dive deeper in the snow and leads to falling forward, head first, over your tips. For this reason, beginning powder skiers tend to keep their weight back on their heels. However, this is not good either. As explained above, this requires more energy and makes it difficult to turn.

The proper forward/backward weight balance in powder is with your weight centered over the ski. You should feel some weight on your heels while your shins simultaneously push against the tongues of your boots **[Figure 51]**. Precisely how much weight can be brought forward cannot be specifically defined. Let your weight press forward, pressing your shins against your boot tops, as long as your ski tips don't dive deep. If they dive, you have put too much weight forward; if they don't dive, continue pushing your shins against the boot tops. As a rule, you should always feel some pressure of your shins against your boot tops in powder, just as on pack.

On steep slopes, the tendency is to sit too far back. You start to feel your skis get ahead of your body and it's hard to catch up. On steep slopes, to maintain your weight in the center of your foot you must increase the forward lean of your body to keep your body centered over your skis. At first this is hard to do because you feel like you are going to do a somersault over your tips. On steep slopes your weight tends to fall back on your heels, and your shins pull back from your boot tops. Don't let this happen. Regardless of the steepness, it is important to maintain your shins pushing against your boot tops. Once you become accustomed to the feeling of skiing steep slopes with your weight a little forward you will discover that it is easier on your thigh muscles. You are using gravity to help center yourweight over your skis. **Note:** If you find that you must put all your weight on your heels to prevent your ski tips from diving below the snow, your bindings may be mounted too far forward and should be adjusted backwards. Moving them back just one cm will often make a big difference.

On gentle slopes the reverse is true. You tend to put too much weight forward on gentle pitches. It's harder to keep some weight back on your heels because it strains your thigh muscles. You can't use gravity to help as you can on steep slopes.

3. Complete turns by carving: On packed slopes, turns can be completed by following the side of the skis as they skid and sideslip or by following the tips of the skis as they carve on their curved edges. In powder you usually don't have two choices; the skis won't move sideways, won't sideslip, and seldom skid. There is too much resistance to sideways (lateral) motion by the deep snow. In powder, turns must be completed by following the tips of the skis; following the curve in the skis created by your weight on flexible skis. This makes the completion phase of powder turns long radius and wide arc. If you need a short radius turn, it must be created in the initiation phase of the turn by down-UP pressure release and pivoting both feet, because the completion phase is always a gradual turn.

Carving is defined as following the direction of a curved ski. The term carving is generally used when talking about packed snow; it seldom is used in describing powder skiing. The term carving in deep powder can be confusing: How can you carve when the entire bottom of the ski is weighted rather than just the edge of the ski? On pack, when a flexible ski lies flat, it has no curve in it. To carve, the ski must be set on its edge so the tip and tail can hold the slope while the waist of the ski is suspended in air. The ski is then shaped in a curve by the pressure of your weight.

In deep powder, as on pack, carving is still defined as following the path of a curved ski, but the mechanism of creating the curve in the ski is different. In powder, the curve has nothing to do with the tip and tail suspending the waist. In powder, the curve in the ski is created by your weight on the ski, whether the ski is lying flat or on its side, because the ski is floating on the powder in either case. Rolling the ski onto its side results in the bottom of the ski continuing to press against the snow.

From the skier's point of view, it isn't necessary to know that the curve in a ski is achieved differently in powder than on pack. Although the mechanism for carving is different, the action is the same: Knee angulation. Rolling your knees to the side puts the skis on their sides ready to carve the end of a turn whether on pack or in deep powder.

Steepness of slope

Gentle slopes: Fresh powder on slopes with gentle pitches is a skier's delight. The powder slows you enough so you need very little edging for speed control. Long radius turns can be made by a down-UP motion for a moment of pressure release, pivoting your feet a few degrees, and angulating your knees, just a little, to carve the end of the turn.

An alternative to down-UP pressure release and knee angulation is to bank each turn with your upper body. You can begin with a gentle, slow, relaxed down-up motion and move your upper body inward, towards the center of the turn. This banks your skis at the beginning of the turn. You then hold this banked position through a wide radius turn. After the skis cross the fall line and head uphill, the next turn commences. By going down-UP and moving your hips and upper body inward again, banking in the other direction, the action is repeated. With practice, you can ski to a regular slow rhythm of either down-UP, pivot, carve; down-UP, pivot, carve; etc.; or you can set up a slow rhythm of down-UP, inward lean, carve; it permits you to rest your thigh muscles which work a lot harder in powder than on pack. On gentle slopes with deep powder, just rolling your knees to bank and make long radius turns is adequate to control speed. Sharp, short radius turns may slow you down too much so you lose your momentum and have trouble turning at all.

Steep slopes: A very steep slope with soft powder is easier to control than is hardpack on the same slope. On packed snow, the steeper the slope the more difficult it is to set your edges. Powder gives you a soft surface that lets your edges hold better and makes them more effective. Powder also lets the entire bottoms of your skis support you and prevent you from skidding. The consistency and resistance of powder pushing against your boot and leg is another aide in slowing you down.

The technics described in the chapter on steep slopes (Chapter 11) apply to powder as well as pack. Turns must be initiated by pressure release and pivoting both feet. While the resistance of powder to sideways movement of the skis makes skidding and sideslipping difficult in powder, it is usually possible to pivot both skis under the snow if your rotation forces are prepared and working together. On very steep slopes, once you have some momentum, you may also skid and sideslip as the forces of gravity from the steepness are strong enough to overcome the resistance of the powder to sideways movement.

In light powder, you can generate enough rotational power to turn your skis in a short radius turn by keeping your shoulders facing downhill (anticipation), releasing pressure, and pivoting your feet. However, in heavy powder, this may not be enough. To get more rotational power, you must rotate your hips and sometimes your shoulders, too. In heavy powder, it is impossible to wedel down a steep slope making turns in rapid succession; you must do it one turn at a time. Since you use shoulder rotation to help you pivot, you can't use your shoulders for anticipation. The sequence of actions for turning in heavy powder on steep slopes is:

1. Exaggerate your down-UP pressure release (unweighting)
2. As you rise up, lift the pole of your outside arm (the one not being used to pole plant) and raise your outside hip (hip angulation or hip projection)
3. Pivot your outside hip and outside shoulder toward the fall line (See Figure 38, hip projection)
4. Roll your knees into the hill and finish the turn by carving

Hopefully, this will provide enough turning power to get your skis around to face in the opposite direction.

If using hip and shoulder rotation won't turn you fast enough, the only other thing to add is vigorous down-UP unweighting by planting both poles simultaneously in front of you and lifting your heels out of the snow.

Part III

Extras

Chapter 14
Difficult Conditions

Ice
Crust
Crud

Ice

It is difficult to impossible to ski well on ice. Just as soft powder is the skier's ideal for its reliability in providing excellent edge control, ice is the skier's nemesis because it is too hard to permit good edge control. If you can't depend on edging for speed control you can't ski comfortably.

In the United States, skiers from New England and New York have much more experience with ice than skiers from Colorado or Utah. If you ask Eastern skiers where they prefer to ski you'll find it's no contest; they all prefer the West. Why? Because it's ice in the East and soft snow in the West. No one likes ice; it's too hard to control.

Unfortunately, even in the beautiful West, you will one day have to cope with ice. While you won't enjoy it as much as soft snow there are a few things you can do to **survive** on ice. First, equipment is important. Very sharp edges and stiff skis work best. Sharp edges have a better chance of holding on ice than dull edges. Stiff skis hold an edge with more security than flexible skis. However, at times even the best skis don't work.

On ice, certain technics of turning and stopping are more effective than others. The general principle is to avoid skidding as much as possible. Below are some guidelines to help you deal with ice.

1. Transfer weight from ski to ski slowly and cautiously. Sudden and abrupt weight shifts should be avoided as should quick twisting of your shoulders. On ice all movements produce exaggerated responses and are diffi-

cult to control. Therefore, ski gently and lightly; use subtle movements as if you are trying to disguise them.

2. Steering your turns as much as possible is good technic on ice. Steering lets you keep your weight on both feet and exert gradual pressure on your edges to turn.

3. Ski on your edges as much as possible. Emphasize knee angulation and hip angulation, but avoid banking as banking requires larger movements of your upper body from side to side.

4. Increase and decrease pressure on your skis slowly and deliberately. Avoid completely releasing pressure because when you reapply pressure to your feet, there is a greater tendency to skid without control.

5. Stem turns work better than pivoted parallel turns on ice. Keep some weight on each ski all the time. Once a ski starts skidding, that is moving sideways, it is hard to check it on ice. Carve the completion of your turns as much as possible to avoid skidding. You won't always be successful but it's worth trying.

6. Weight your heels a little more than your toes. Don't try to keep your shin pushing hard against your boot top as you do when skiing soft snow. Let yourself sit back a little to avoid over-weighting your ski tips which let your tails pivot quickly in a skid. By keeping your tails weighted you will help reduce skidding which is hard to stop. Another way to feel this is by pushing your feet forward thereby extending (straightening) your ankles.

7. Turn where there is a patch of snow rather than on sheer ice. There are usually snowy spots on all icy slopes; try to identify them and turn there. On icy slopes, the best place to find snow is on the ascending side of a mogul (the side you ski first). This side of the mogul also helps you slow down because it is sloping uphill. If there is any soft snow on that slope, it is apt to be on the upside of moguls because most skiers avoid turning there rendering it less skied.

Crust

No one likes to ski crust because it is unreliable, undependable and filled with surprises. Unfortunately, if you like to ski powder, you will run into crust. As powder ages, the wind and sun cause freezing and thawing which turns the soft powder surface into a frozen sheet of firm packed snow, often with soft snow beneath it. Crust is treacherous because it can appear smooth and soft so you fail to alter your speed and rhythm before it's too late.

The consistency of crust is unpredictable. It can be very firm and tough for a distance, then become soft and breakable. Variations from breakable to unbreakable crust occur frequently in any given run over crust. You must be prepared for frequent changes but have no way to predict when they will occur.

Unbreakable crust is easier to handle than breakable crust because your skis stay on top of the crust where they are more maneuverable. If skis break through the crust they rest on a bed of soft snow where they have difficulty sliding and pivoting. They are stuck, immobile, and you have little ability to control them.

Unbreakable crust is skied in much the same way as ice. Use stem turns, minimize all movements, and avoid extending or straightening your knees abruptly. The later movement can increase pressure on your skis to the point where they break through the crust. Try to ski slowly through unbreakable crust because you never know when your skis will break the crust and slow you down abruptly. Continuous short turns are better than long traverses to help control your speed. Transfer your weight slowly and delicately; set your edges cautiously and minimally to avoid breaking the crust. Distribute your weight as evenly as possible between the two skis and when stem turning transfer just enough weight to turn. A ski with half your weight on it is less likely to break through the crust than one with all of your weight.

If the gentle movements still don't prevent you from breaking through the crust, you must change your technic to handle breakable crust. Parallel turns with down-UP pressure release can be as effective as any method. Maintain your weight in the center of your skis or a little back to prevent diving over your ski tips if you stop abruptly. Turn by planting your ski pole, lifting up, and pivoting your feet. As you reapply pressure to your skis you have two choices: You can flex your knees to soften your reweighting in the hope that your skis will not break through; or you can extend your knees firmly, trying to break the crust with authority. Once broken, continue doing short turns until you reach a stretch of crust that doesn't break. You'll usually find one down the slope.

Crud

Crud is broken snow, crust, or ice that has occurred from various disturbances such as avalanches, previous skiers, extreme melting and freezing, or even snow falling from tree tops. Stay on your edges as much as possible and reduce your speed. If you run into a large clump of snow, you can be thrown and badly injured if you are skiing fast. Jumping with down-UP pressure release, using one or two poles, may be the best way to facilitate turns. Few people ski these well. Get over these areas as quickly as possible and remember that everyone else has trouble here, too.

Chapter 15

Equipment

Boots
Skis
Bindings
Poles
Device to reduce thigh and knee stress

While good equipment won't make you a good skier, improper equipment can make skiing a lot harder. Technology introduces improved equipment every few years. These changes can make skiing a little easier, but technology hasn't changed how the skier uses basic skills. Below are some guidelines and practical suggestions regarding equipment.

Boots

Comfort: The primary features of a good ski boot are comfort and holding the foot in the boot with a minimum of movement inside the boot, particularly, minimum lifting of your heel upwards when you initiate a turn. The heel must be held snugly in the boot; there should be ample room for the toes; and most good boots will give you a little forward lean.

Double socks: Boots should feel comfortable, that is, no pressure or painful spots after wearing them for a few hours. Today, boots are designed to hold the foot snugly. You do not have to wear heavy socks with them; these will not keep your feet warmer. Have the boot fitted with a single pair of thin socks. When skiing, do not wear double socks. A tight boot, made tighter by a double pair of socks, will make your foot colder because the increased pressure against your foot squeezes out the blood supply to the skin of your foot.

Flexibility: Flexibility in a boot is one of the comfort features. Flexible boots are usually more comfortable than stiff ones. However, the more the flexibility, the slower will be the response of the boot to movements of your foot. Your goal in skiing is to transfer motion of your legs to the ski. The boot is the transfer agent in this process. Leg movements are first transferred to the boot which in turn relays them to the ski. If the boot is very soft, small foot and leg movements will be absorbed by the flexibility so very little of the movement reaches the ski and the ski responds minimally, if at all. In contrast, stiff boots do a better job of getting quick and appropriate responses from small leg movements.

At the novice and intermediate level, select flexibility and comfort in a boot as most of your movements will be large enough to get good responses from the skis. As you advance to higher levels and begin to use small subtle movements in your legs, you may wish a stiffer boot. The only way to know what's right for you is to demonstrate boots of different stiffness. In general, for recreational skiers a flexible boot will work quite well; leave the very stiff boots for the racers.

Fixed heel: A fixed heel is the single most important feature of the boot. Many boots are designed with an adjustable cable over the ankle. When the cable is tightened it holds your heel down so it won't come up when you release pressure. You can test this feature in the store with a boot on and buckled up by actually placing the boot in a ski binding and leaning far forward. Your heel should not rise up more than a couple of millimeters.

Length and Toe space: Toe space, on the other hand, need not be tight. You should be able to wiggle your toes inside the boot. Your big toe should not hit the tip of the boot. If it does, you run the risk of getting a painful, blue toenail on your big toe. This results from the toenail hitting the end of the boot when skiing hard and rupturing small blood vessels under the big toenail. Wearing a boot a half size longer will usually cure this problem.

Forward lean: Forward lean is a desired feature in a boot. This helps you comfortably ski with a little forward flexion in your ankle all the time. In turn this requires you to balance this forward weight shift by flexing your knees to bring your weight back to center. A good ski position is one in which your knees and ankles are both in a little flexion, letting your seat drop over your heels. Forward lean in a boot helps you do this painlessly.

Cants: Cants are an important feature in fitting any boot. A cant is a wedge, usually placed inside your boot (but can also be placed on your ski), to compensate for unequal balance between the inside and outside of your foot. Most people carry more of their weight on the outside edges of their feet. You can tell this by observing the heels of your street shoes. If they are more worn on the outside edges it means that you carry more of your weight on this side of your foot. In an unmodified ski boot, standing straight with your feet together will put most of your weight on the outside edges of the skis. As you ski, this mal-distribution of weight on your skis will make your skis separate. It becomes hard to keep your skis near each other when parallel skiing.

To compensate for unequal weight distribution in your foot, a wedge of material (a cant) is placed in your boot with the wide end of the wedge beneath the side of your foot where there is less weight, usually the inside edge. Today, many boots come with cants already built into the inside edge of the boot. However, this may or may not be the correct amount of wedging for you. This can and should be tested in a boot store. If your feet require cants, get them. The small investment is well worth it. On the ski slope, one way to test whether or not you need cants is to ski a straight line on a gentle flat slope or trail with your feet touching each other. If your skis tend to drift apart or run into each other you should have your feet and boots checked for cants.

Skis

Length: The longer the ski, the more stable it is at high speeds; the shorter the ski, the easier it is to turn. In general you want as short a ski as possible to make turning easier. On the other hand, too short a ski results in the ski wobbling and chattering as your speed increases. The general rule of thumb is to start with a short length ski and increase your length if your skis chatter or wiggle at the speed you like to use. If the skis feel stable at your speed, don't go longer; either keep that length or test a shorter length.

While your height has nothing to do with ski length, it is a practical guide in finding a starting length. Beginning with a ski a little longer than your height, you can lengthen or shorten your ski length depending on how it feels at speed. Once you've reached the intermediate level, only you can tell, by trial and error, how long a ski is correct for you.

Your body weight is a more important factor in ski length than your height. Heavier people need a longer length for stability than lighter people.

Side-cut: The ski's side-cut is the curve in the side of the ski from tip to tail (See Figure 1, page 5). There are three standard side-cuts in skis: Downhill, giant slalom, and slalom. The three terms refer to the type of race for which they are designed. The downhill ski has virtually no side-cut, the curve in the side is virtually a straight line. This gives the downhill ski a little more surface area to provide more stability at high speeds. The downhill race has very few turns so there is little need for side-cut. The slalom ski has the greatest amount of side-cut to permit sharper turns. The giant slalom has some curve but not as much as the slalom ski. This is appropriate for giant slalom because it combines the downhill principle of speed with the slalom principle of frequent turns. For recreational skiers, the slalom cut is the best choice because it makes carving turns easier.

Parabolic skis: The parabolic ski design has made 21st century skiing easier. The parabolic ski is a ski with a wider tip and wider tail than the skis made prior to 1990. This provides two features: 1) The ski has a greater total surface area, thus providing greater stability than standard skis of the same length. This permits you to use a ski of shorter length than you had used previously. And 2) the ski has greater side-cut, making turning easier when the ski is rolled onto its inside edge.The combination of the same stability with a shorter length ski plus the easier turning with a greater side-cut has made the parabolic ski quite popular. However, you must still use the same basic skills on parabolic skis as you did on your old standard skis.

Width: Width provides stability to a ski. The wider the ski, the more stable at speeds. However, as a ski gets wider, it becomes harder to set on its edge. Therefore, a ski must be wide enough for stability but stay narrow enough so it can easily be rolled onto an edge. Width is not a critical feature in a ski, except in powder where a wider ski provides a better ride and more stability. On packed snow, a narrower ski is a little easier to turn and edge than a wide one. As mentioned in Chapter 13: Powder, very wide skis make skiing easier in difficult snow conditions, such as crud and broken powder.

Flexibility: A stiff ski has minimal carving ability, but provides greater stability at speeds. If you ski fast on smooth, gentle slopes you may prefer the stiffer ski for its security and steadiness at higher speeds. Downhill racers prefer a stiff ski. More flexibility gives a ski greater curve when carving. This makes turning easier, skiing bumps easier, and especially skiing powder a lot easier. Most recreational skiers prefer the more flexible ski.

Responsiveness: The ability of a ski to snap back when you release the pressure on it is the ski's responsiveness. Technological advances in ski construction have made big changes in the ability of the modern ski to respond quickly to small pressure changes. Responsiveness is determined by the materials in the ski, particularly in the core of the ski. Some materials respond quicker than others which is one of the major differences in skis. A ski's responsiveness can only be determined by skiing on it.

Torsion: A ski's torsion is the degree of flexibility, or twist, in the side of the shovel of the ski. Torsion is most helpful in bumps. As your ski tip hits the side of a bump it can remain rigid and jar you, indicating little torsion; or it can bend a little on its long axis and absorb some of the sideways pressure to bend, indicating more torsion. In contrast, when cruising at higher speeds, you want the shovel of the ski to be stiff, with little or no torsion, so the edge will hold without yielding to provide a steady and secure feeling when performing wide arc turns.

Demonstrate skis before buying: Once you reach

the intermediate level, the best way to select the right ski for you is to try it before you buy it. Rent a demonstrator pair of skis and ski on them for a day. If you can, try two or three different skis on the same day. Many ski areas have rental programs in their ski shops that will let you ski a run or two on one pair of skis and then exchange them for another demonstrator pair. You can sometimes do this several times in one day.

No ideal ski for all conditions: There is no such thing as one ski that is perfect in every condition. Many skiers have at least two pair, one for cruising and one for bumps. To this you can add a third pair for deep powder: Skis that are soft, a little wider, and have bindings mounted a cm behind the binding position of your hardpack skis.

Bindings

Since safety bindings were introduced about 1960, technology in bindings has made significant progress; and progress will continue. The ideal binding will release when you exert too much pressure on it in the wrong direction, but will not release indiscriminately when you hit a bump or trough. Bindings that release too easily can be as dangerous as those that don't release soon enough. Most binding manufacturers offer a choice of features at increasing prices. It is a good investment to buy a versatile binding. The best bindings are designed with sophisticated adjustments for quick load adjustments so they can begin to release when they are challenged with a severe twist or load, but can then return to center if the load is not sustained, avoiding the unnecessary release. At higher speeds, these bindings have the built-in ability to distinguish between transient forces from jars and impacts of the slope, which do not require release, and the more sustained forces of a fall or twist which do demand release.

Poles

Length: The ideal pole length is related to your height, more so than your ski length. In general, the distance between the basket and top of the pole handle should be the distance from the floor to your elbow, plus 5-10 cm, as measured while you stand erect with your knees extended. If you have a tendency to ski with your legs too straight, using poles 5 cm shorter may help you flex your knees more. If your tendency is to ski with your knees too flexed, poles 5 cm longer may help you ski more upright.

Straps: Straps on your ski poles should be regarded as an attachment to help you hang your poles on a rack when you stop for lunch. Although many skiers wear them around their wrists, this can be a dangerous habit. If you fall sideways burying your ski pole beneath you, you can injure your thumb or shoulder because the pole strap traps your arm, preventing it from releasing. Therefore, either use safety straps which let your pole fall away from your arm or don't use the straps at all.

Should you elect to wear your straps on your hands anyway, it is better to wear them across your palm instead of over your wrist. However, in trees, everyone agrees that you should release your pole straps completely from either your wrist or hand to avoid injury. This occurs when the pole is caught and held by a branch or stump. If your pole is fixed to your wrist, shoulder dislocation can result.

Weight: Poles should be as light in weight as possible. Poles are to assist in balance and stability during the moment of pressure release when your skis are unweighted. The rest of the time they can be a burden. The lighter the burden the easier it is to ski.

Device to reduce thigh and knee stress

Since the introduction of safety bindings, there have been no major innovations in ski equipment. In 1991, a new device called CADS was introduced to help take the load off your knees and quadriceps (muscles on top of your thighs where you feel burning when skiing properly). By use of a rubber spring fixed to the heel of your boot, a climber's thigh harness with an attached string, and a pulley on a rod, it has been possible to reduce the weight on your quadriceps muscles by bending your knees. The more your seat drops, the more the spring stretches and the more the force builds to pick your seat back up. The device helps you keep your weight forward. For people with bad knees and for people whose legs tend to give out early in the day or early in a run, the CADS device provides significant relief.

A word of caution: There is a risk to using CADS. When wearing the device, it is harder to catch your balance when you lose it. As a result, a skier is more prone to injury with a fall.

Chapter 16

Appendix of exercises on the slopes & before a mirror

Knee angulation and shoulders downhill
Wedeln exercise
Sideslipping exercise–Garlands
Knee angulation in front of a mirror
Pressure release (Unweighting) exercises
Leg retraction

For your convenience, this appendix contains in one place the exercises described in Chapters 3-6. Some of these exercises are for the ski slopes; others are to practice at home, in front of a mirror.

Knee angulation and shoulders downhill

Traverse a gentle hill. Rotate and hold your shoulders and upper body facing down the fall line all the time. Feel your downhill shoulder pulled back, and at the same time, keep your poles in front of your body. Every few seconds, angulate your knees into the hill and feel your abdominal muscles tighten as your skis turn further uphill, while your upper body remains facing down the fall line. As you feel yourself slow down, de-angulate your knees to stop turning uphill, and traverse further. You will feel partial relaxation of your abdominal muscles. Repeat this sequence several times; knee angulation into the hill slows you down while reducing knee angulation lets you speed up. Concentrate on the tight feeling of your abdominal muscles as you twist your shoulders to face downhill while your skis move at a right angle to your upper body. This exercise is also good practice for knee angulating. After traversing the width of the slope, turn in the opposite direction and practice the same thing the other way.

Wedeln exercise

On a gentle, flat slope, ski straight down the fall line with your poles held in both hands in front of you.

Establish a wedeln rhythm of:

1. down-UP pressure release (unweight) with quick, short lifts of your seat and
2. pivot both feet in one direction
3. simultaneousl move your poles in the opposite direction, still holding your poles straight in front of your body and your body fixed facing down the falline.
4. continuously repeat these actions to a regular rhythm

In performing this exercise, you feel like you are doing "The Twist" on a dance floor with both feet twisting in one direction and your hips, arms, and shoulders twisting in the opposite direction. There is a asynchronism between the upper and lower body.

Sideslipping exercise–Garlands

Some simple exercises on the slopes can help you get the feel of edge control by knee angulation. Controlled sideslipping is the first. This is done by standing on a moderately steep pitch with your skis facing across the hill. Try it on a mogul.

1. Flex your knees.
2. Begin sliding sideways, downhill, by rolling your knees away from the hill (down the fall line), so the skis come close to lying parallel to the snow.
3. After sliding for a few feet, check your slide by rolling your knees into the hill. This rolls the edges of your skis into the snow to slow down and eventually stop.
4. Repeat the two maneuvers of rolling your knees away from and into the hill to permit the skis to slide downhill and to stop.
5. Most of your weight will fall onto the downhill ski, which is fine. Actually, sideslipping is easier if the uphill ski has no weight at all on it. Let the uphill knee touch the downhill knee, so the two skis move in unison.

Another exercise is to traverse a slope, alternately rolling your edges into the hill, then releasing them. Each time you increase the degree of knee angulation uphill, the skis will turn uphill. Each time you release the edges, the skis will straighten out (See Figure 24, Garlands, page 56).

Knee angulation in front of a mirror

If you are unfamiliar with knee angulation you can experiment with it in front of a mirror in warmth and comfort. You needn't be on skis to learn this but you can put them on if you wish. Begin by dropping your seat over your heels in a knee-flexed position. Next, roll your knees to one side. Note that your ankles and feet have rolled to the same side and you are standing on the sides of your feet. If skis are attached to your feet, the skis will follow your feet and rest on their edges too. Wearing ski boots when you try this will show you that the boot stiffens the ankle joint so it won't bend when the knees angulate. The rolling of the knees is transferred immediately to the feet.

Pressure release (Unweighting) exercises

There are some exercises that can help you learn pressure release. One of the easiest is to plant both poles in the snow a little in front of you. Leaning on both poles, flex both knees and quickly lift your seat hard enough to lift both heels off the ground. The tails of the skis will lift off the ground, too. The feeling you experience at the moment your heels are off the ground is the feeling of weightlessness. Remember it. This is the same feeling you want to experience when releasing pressure to turn.

Leg retraction

Leg retraction can be felt indoors by supporting your weight with extended arms on the backs of two chairs. In order to lift both feet simultaneously off the ground, you must tighten your belly muscles and lift your knees up. Notice that it is easier to perform if your knees are bent. As a matter of fact, flexed knees are a necessary prerequisite to leg retraction (See Figure 34, leg retraction, page 76).

Glossary of Ski Terms

Alpine skiing Downhill skiing

Angulation Bending one or more joints of the body

Knee Angulation (also called cranking) Bending the knee joint sideways to set the ski on an edge. This action of the knee is possible only when the knee joint is flexed. Knee angulation is the most important mechanism.

Hip Angulation Pushing the hips uphill and leaning the shoulders downhill to set the skis on their edges.

Anticipation Facing the upper body (shoulders and head) downhill before a turn is made.

Banking Leaning inward against centrifugal force. Banking is a form of edge control as it results in setting the skis on their inside edges. Banking on skis is similar to banking on a bicycle.

Camber The flexibility of a ski. The upward curve in a ski when lying flat. When the ski is set on its edge and the body's weight pushes against the center of the ski, the ski's camber curve reverses. This is called reverse camber. The ski's reverse camber is used to carve a turn.

Carving Completing a turn by following the arc produced in the ski when it is edged and weighted. The carved turn is one that follows the direction in which the ski tip is pointing. The opposite of a carved turn is a skidded turn in which the turn is led by the side of the ski rather than the tip.

Checking Reducing speed by a quick edgeset. Used for slowing down and stopping.

Christy A parallel turn that ends with a skid. The term was born in the town of Christiana, now called Oslo, in Norway. This term is seldom used in modern skiing.

Cranking The same as knee angulation. Rolling the knees to the side to change the direction of the ski by edging.

Edge Change A method of initiating a parallel turn by switching from one set of edges to the other set. This changes the direction in which the skis are pointing.

Extension Straightening out a flexed joint. When controlling pressure, extending or straightening the knee joint increases the pressure on the ski to achieve stronger edging.

Fall line The shortest and steepest path down a hill.

Flexion Bending a joint. A correct ski stance will include flexion of knee, ankle, and hip joints.

Foot twist or swivel Rotating the feet to initiate a parallel turn.

Herringbone Technic for walking uphill with ski tips pointing upward.

Hip Projection A form of hip rotation in which the outside hip is lifted up and rotated in the direction of the turn. Elevating the hip flattens the skis against the slope to make it a little easier to pivot them.

Inside leg or ski The leg or ski nearest the center of a turn.

Lateral Sideways. A lateral movement is a movement to the side.

Leverage The effect of a skier's weight when it is transferred ahead of or behind the center of the ski.

Jetting A quick thrust of the feet and legs resulting from the release of stretched muscles. Flexing the knees deeply and angulating them to the side stretches the extensor muscles of the legs. When releasing pressure relaxes these muscles, their rebound thrusts the feet forward.

Leg Retraction A method of pressure release by tightening the abdominal and back muscles and lifting the knees upward.

Nordic Skiing Cross country skiing

Outside leg or ski The leg or ski away from the center of a turn.

Parallel Turn A turn initiated by changing the direction of both skis simultaneously.

Platform The position of tight compression of the legs produced by both knee flexion and knee angulation. This provides a stable springboard from which to launch a turn.

Pressure release Same as unweighting.

Pre-turn Also called counter turn, is turning the skis uphill just prior to turning downhill.

Rotation Turning the body around its long axis. The body's long axis is comparable to a flagpole running from the top of the head to a point between the two feet. A twisting movement of the feet, knees, hips, or shoulders will turn the body around its long axis.

Side-cut or Side-camber The curve in the side of the ski produced by the tip and tail being wider than the mid-section of the ski. The side-cut permits the ski to carve on a packed slope when weighted and properly edged.

Sideslipping Lateral movement of the ski. The side of the ski leads the ski straight down the fall line.

Sideslipping is performed by releasing the edges to partially flatten the bottoms of the skis against the slope.

Skidding Completing a turn by combining sideslipping with rotation of the skis. The tails of the skis slip faster than the tips, causing the tails to rotate around the tips. In skidding, the turn is led by the side of the ski, whereas in carving the turn is led by the tip of the ski.

Snowplow See Wedge below.

Steering Changing the direction of the skis gradually by applying the forces of both knee angulation and foot rotation without releasing pressure from the skis.

Stem Turn Derived from the German word stemmen, meaning to push against or brace. The stem turn is a one-legged turn performed by transferring weight from one leg to the other. Stemming is initiated by pushing the tail of one ski outward so the ski is pointing in the new direction, rolling that ski onto its inside edge, then transferring weight to it.

Traversing Traveling across a hill perpendicular to the fall line without lateral slippage.

Torsion The longitudinal flexibilty of a ski.

Unweighting Releasing pressure from your skis by reducing the weight on your feet.

Wedeln The German word for wiggle. Wedeln is a technic of turning rapidly in which the turning action is performed by the lower half of the body while the upper half remains facing downhill.

Wedge or Snowplow Position of the skis with the tips together and the tails apart. This position is used primarily for slowing down or stopping on narrow trails by setting the skis on their inside edges.

Weighting Placing body weight on one or both feet. This places pressure on the ski which enables the edged ski to bite into the snow and change direction, decelerate, or stop.

Weight Transfer Shifting weight from one place to another. In skiing, weight is transferred in two ways. It can be shifted from foot to foot, or shifted from one part of the foot to another part (See leverage).

NOTES

NOTES

NOTES

About the Author

R.J. Sanders, a Denver surgeon, was a member of th Colorado Doctors Ski Patrol for many years. A graduate o the University of Michigan, Dr. Sanders has been on th teaching faculty of the University of Colorado Medica School since 1960. In this book he has combined his back ground in anatomy and teaching with his years of experienc skiing in the mountains of Colorado.